TEACHERS
FIRST

A Guide to
Avoiding and Overcoming
Burnout
in the Classroom

Carman Murray

Cover by: Kristina Edstrom
Edited by: Lexi Mohney

PEAK PRESS

An Imprint for GracePoint Publishing (www.GracePointPublishing.com)

GracePoint Matrix, LLC
624 S. Cascade Ave, Suite 201
Colorado Springs, CO 80903
www.GracePointMatrix.com
Email: Admin@GracePointMatrix.com

SAN # 991-6032

Library of Congress Control Number: 2023943834

ISBN: (Paperback) 978-1-961347-08-3
eISBN: 978-1-961347-09-0

Books may be purchased for educational, business, or sales promotional use.
For bulk order requests and price schedule contact:
Orders@GracePointPublishing.com

Praise for *Teachers First*

Carman's book, *Teachers First,* is more than just inspiring words and stories; it's personal, and it's practical. By sharing her journey as an educator and a leader, and weaving it together with practical tips, strategies and (gasp!) actual homework for you to do… she creates a "must read" for teachers and educators that want to move past the things that wear us out and into a place of abundance and thriving. This an easily digestible guide to resilience for you, your family, and the students you work with!

Ian Tyson (he/him)
Speaker, Author,
Silver Lining Prospector

I loved this book! In *Teachers First,* Carman Murray presents a pragmatic approach to building a resilient teacher. It shows teachers real examples of what burnout looks, sounds, and feels like. She provides both a tool kit to success and a narrative to go with it. Carman exemplifies her sentiment that "There is a balance between vulnerability and professionalism."

Nick Foley MA,
Organizational Leadership

You matter. It's a lesson every educator teaches but many can struggle to learn. "You matter" is the core principle on which *Teachers First* has been built, and it's a foundation upon which Carman Murray has placed a treasure trove of insights, stories, and strategies that will help any educator create a better, healthier classroom by creating a better, healthier you. More importantly, it reminds you why you deserve it.

Drew Dudley,
Wall Street Journal Bestselling
Author of *This is Day One*

Table of Contents

Foreword

Teachers of all levels and experience now have a roadmap to avoid or reverse burnout.

Carman's book offers simple steps, stories, and strategies. Teachers who experiment more with the practices within will benefit the most. Your students will be equipped with the skills they need most in this digital mania experience that is now childhood. Plus, Carman gets you organized, focused, and on top of your life.

I'm Cate Stillman, an author, coach and global community leader at Club Thrive and Wellness Pro Academy. I'm devoted to integrating ancient wisdom into modern life with my clubs and books (*Body Thrive, Primal Habits, Master of You*). We resolve chronic symptoms, ignite ambition with strategy, and build the skills of collaborative intelligence.

It is immensely fulfilling to see Carman's book. Carman joined us in Yoga Health Coaching (now Wellness Pro Academy) years ago. She excelled and stepped onto our leadership path. She is down-to-earth, is playful, and helps other people feel comfortable in their own skin.

The exercises in Carman's book get you thinking about what is really going on in your life. Right now. When you're in the whirlwind of the every day, you may miss signs of burnout... which will have serious consequences down the road. Teachers who come across this book will be able to reverse burnout and rejuvenate. They will regain a relaxed present ease at work. Her nonjudgmental tone engages you in self-evaluation that propels the change you want in your life.

As you go through this book, don't just read. Do the exercises. Write out the journal entries. You'll have insights that will change not just your classroom, but also your life. You'll develop true self-care, smarter boundaries, and proactive routines. Plus, you'll train your students on how to show up and grow in your classroom.

I recommend this book to all the teachers I know who report for duty day in and day out. From identifying any of your signs of burnout to building your support team, Carman guides you to take a moment, check in with yourself, and take aligned action.

Implementing small steps will shift your mindset, your sleep, your diet, and your sanity! Thanks, Carman, for creating the guide for teachers around the world.

Cate Stillman
Author, Coach, and
Global Community Leader

What's in It for Me?

You may be wondering why a teacher like you would want to read a book about being a teacher. Perhaps you are the fully tenured one who is eyeballing retirement, or maybe you are just starting or restarting your classroom journey. Either way, this book is for you. By reading this book, you will gain a fresh perspective on what your life *can* look like, as well as learn how to show up both at home and school with the knowledge that *you truly matter*.

In our day-to-day lives, teachers often compare themselves to others and assume others are doing better or have more than they do. However, this situation is not necessarily true. By reading this book, you will begin to understand and implement small steps which will shift your mindset and allow you to celebrate where you are *while* continuing to pursue your life goals and dreams.

It is important to note the "right" answer for someone else is unlikely the exact right answer for you. As a unique human being, it is essential to give yourself the grace and permission to explore what works best, using both failures and successes to guide you to the next step.

This book provides a roadmap, offering simple steps, stories, and strategies to inspire you to take action and experiment with ideas in your classroom and personal life. You will also gain tools to teach your students, equipping them with the skills they need to be even more successful in your classroom, school, and their lives in general. Each time you pick up this book, it will serve as a reminder that *you* matter, and how you treat yourself and those around you reflects what you are modeling for the world.

How to Use This Book

To begin with, I recommend reading the "Teacher First" section. It is important to understand how we can step up as leaders before we ask others to do the same. As you read this section, choose one to three actions to add to your life to improve health and wellness. Make sure to choose at least one action which is almost too easy, so it is impossible for you not to do it. This will boost your confidence and inspiration to break free from the perfectionist mindset. When implementing these changes, use the Kaizen approach, gradually implementing small steps instead of trying to do everything all at once.

As you continue reading, take note of small action steps to implement in your classroom. When you feel overwhelmed, focus on self-care until you are ready to add another new step. Use the section titles to guide you in choosing what to read next. Feel free to identify where you want to grow as a teacher and focus on that section, keeping in mind that you do not have to read the book cover to cover.

Consider how you want students to feel in your classroom. There are many different personalities and learning styles, and it's still your responsibility to see your students' full potential. What if there are some traditional beliefs about education, students, and teachers that may be holding you back? It's important to revisit and perhaps grow to meet the changing needs of those in the room.

Moving into the next section, the focus is on resetting your and your students' mindset. Determine the atmosphere you want in your classroom, and as the leader, take steps to create that environment. Choose one activity to add in for a month and practice the new activity daily. This will help shift the mindset and atmosphere of your classroom, so everyone can show up at their best.

It is important to keep in mind that not every idea presented in this book may be a good fit for you, your grade level, or your school. When you come across an idea which doesn't resonate with you or isn't practical in your setting, it's okay to let it go and continue reading to find ideas which do work. The goal is to find small, actionable steps to implement in your life and classroom to help you grow as a teacher and create a positive learning environment for your students.

Introduction

As a retired teacher, I wrote this book with the intention of giving back to the teaching community. Looking back on my years in the classroom, there are many moments which make me proud, but also many things I would do differently now with the benefit of hindsight. Since I cannot go back, I am sharing my journey in the hope you might take better care of yourself, connect more deeply with your students, and understand the profound impact you have on the lives of young people as a teacher.

Throughout this book, I share my own struggles, challenges, wins, and celebrations as an educator, along with practical suggestions to implement in your own life and classroom. I want you to know that there is a different way to show up in the school environment, one which doesn't have to be overwhelming and exhausting. You have the power to create the kind of experience you want for yourself and your students within the four walls of your classroom.

My ultimate goal is to encourage prioritizing self-care, and then to step into the amazing teacher you are, equipped with the tools to help children live their lives unapologetically as their unique selves. I hope this book inspires and empowers you to become the best version of yourself, both personally and professionally.

Section One

Teacher First

Section One: Introduction

When I was in the classroom, I loved it… most days. On those days, I had a different mindset and energy. Things were going well in my personal life: I had enough sleep regularly, I fed myself nourishing food, and I had time for the just-for-fun things I loved to do. On the tough days, I noticed the ripple effect in all areas. This is true for life in general; why do we not take the extra time to set ourselves up for success and do what makes us feel great?

My big aha moment around this understanding happened when I was up at 5 a.m. daily from Monday to Friday for an hour of yoga and meditation practice before school. Then on the weekend, I didn't do any of those actions which made me feel great. One day, I paused and thought, *What the heck?* I set myself up for success to be able to handle anything for workdays, but not the days I spent with my family. I felt like I was ripping myself off as I wanted to feel incredible on my off days too. Doing my morning routine is something I commit to seven days a week. These days it ranges from ten to thirty minutes, and it sets me up so I can put my best foot forward, no matter what.

Classroom and students first are a common theme when I speak to teachers. They believe they do not have the time to take care of themselves. They say things like:

"Yes, a daily walk or workout would be great! But I don't have the time."

"Yes, a nice lunch to nourish me for the afternoon so I have energy for my family in the evening would be marvelous, but I don't have the time to even think about what to cook, much less the time to do it."

Teaching can easily take over our lives, leaving little time or energy for anything else. However, it's crucial we challenge the mindset that teachers must always put their own well-being aside for the sake of their students. By becoming aware of this pattern, we can take the first steps toward positive change and create a more sustainable and fulfilling career. The question is this: Are you ready to make a change and rewrite your story?

Don't be discouraged if the idea of change feels overwhelming. It's possible to start small and gradually make progress toward a happier, more balanced life. I speak from experience: Going from burnout to feeling amazing is achievable. By prioritizing our well-being, we can show up fully in all aspects of our lives and find true fulfillment. So, keep reading and discover what steps you can take toward a more fulfilling career as an educator.

Chapter 1

Perfection Clouds Awareness

As we navigate life, we break through barriers and beliefs along the way. We are not the same person we were yesterday, last week, or last year. Thank goodness.

Awareness plays a key role in uncovering what we want to shift. Along the way, we have picked up ideas of what life should look and be like. Often these ideals have us striving for perfection. Unfortunately, these are unrealistic and unattainable, and they often have us aiming at or believing in something which is leading us away from our true selves and our dreams.

How Perfection Clouds Awareness

In exploring our awareness of things, perfection can cloud our ability to listen to those subtle signs which let us know we are on the right track. Perfection is often flaunted in our face regularly through all types of media. The false sense of reality often has us shooting for perfection and not celebrating our current accomplishments; do not fall into this. When we are feeling like we are always falling short of excellence, we do not see how amazing we are. The human experience is what we are here for, and it is messy for everyone. Don't fall into the trap of comparing yourself to others and thinking their grass is greener. It is not! Their mess may look different from yours, yet everyone's life is still messy.

What are your goals and ideals? In reading *The Gap and The Gain* by Dan Sullivan and Dr. Benjamin Hardy, I realized I was aiming for the ideal. The ideal of the perfect mom, the perfect wife, the perfect teacher, the perfect daughter, the perfect friend, and so on. There is no attainable perfect or ideal. Yes, we can set goals and reach them, but the ideal which society portrays is not real! And often, this is a conversation we have with ourselves, and no one else knows we are making these comparisons. What is the ideal you have in your own head about being a teacher? Below is mine.

- The ideal teacher...

- Has a clean desk at the end of the day, every day.

- Has marking up to date, daily.

- Does not get frustrated with the students and their lack of effort.

- Never takes work home.

- Has lots of patience with their family at the end of their day.

- Has all the lesson plans completed before they teach the lesson.

- Arrives to work early.

- Is finished with everything and can leave thirty minutes after class.

- Is ready and feels excited each day as students arrive.

- Feels accomplished and does a great job each day.

- Says yes to the extras when asked.

- Does not feel overwhelmed.

- Is on top of their to-do list.

And in contrast the below was my lived experience:

- My desk had papers on it regularly, often layers of them. Thank goodness for colored paper!

- The marking I took home on Friday, hoping to complete, often returned with me on Monday, unfinished.

- Students' lack of effort frustrated me to no end. Sometimes I had to take a breath and walk away, other times I raised my voice, and other times I had amazing patience and understanding.

- I often took work home, and usually it sat at my back door, making me feel guilty I hadn't done it.

- By the time I got home, I was exhausted. My family got what was left of me, which wasn't much. I was impatient with my children and husband.

- I loved project learning, and I had ideas planned out in my head for a few weeks to a month. And often, amazing ideas came up as we learned, and we went with them instead of the planned lesson.

- Lesson plans sometimes were a note on the page, and I went from there.

- I usually arrived early because I love my mornings and I'm most productive.

- Arguing with the photocopier while the bell rang was incredibly frustrating.

- Arriving at class once all my kids were seated was a toss-up as they may be all working or fooling around. (I mostly taught middle school.)

Looking back, I understand the ideals I had of the perfect teacher had no bearing on my ability to engage and teach my students, make them feel welcome in the classroom, and create a safe and brave space for them to learn and grow. My messy desk showed that I cared more for the students struggling than I did about cleaning my desk because that's where I spent my time: with them. The lesson ideas written in my book didn't take away from the engagement and fun we had in our projects as we learned from our experiences. However, the ideals wore me down and sucked my energy because there was often negative self-talk going on in my brain.

Awareness Is the First Step

The focus on baby steps guided by what we are aware of moves us forward, bit by bit. If we allow ourselves to view everything all at one time, we feel like we are failing because we see what we have *not* succeeded in. This feeling is overwhelming, and leaves us not knowing what to do. So, allow yourself to be in awareness and take those tiny steps one at a time to move yourself forward on what is most important to you.

You need to start somewhere and choose to continue, even if you are not doing it how you think it is supposed to look. You may find yourself starting, losing awareness, stopping, and needing to begin again. And that is okay too.

Four years ago, I traveled to Mexico for a retreat, where I learned a lot about myself. When the retreat was finished, I put my notebook on my shelf and didn't look at it until the next year when I went to the retreat again. In reviewing what I wrote the year before, I became aware of how much of what I had set out to do had been accomplished—as well as what hadn't.

Our leader brought that to our attention. She even asked, "Who has not looked at these since you were here last year?"

I did notice I felt some shame and embarrassment as I was one of those people.

Looking back at that moment, the awareness and the uncomfortable feeling convinced me to commit to view each year's notes and plan more often. The journal was still placed on the shelf, but it became a resource, one I looked at more often. I now participate in this course three times a year online, and I'm proud to say I reference my journal monthly, sometimes weekly, as I have my current goals and action steps in it. Because they are my current focus and I reference them, I get less distracted by "shiny objects," courses, and other interruptions which pull me away from my goals and dreams. My current goal of writing this book came out of one of these sessions... what if the next hidden purpose at the very root of me is to write a book? And here I am! If I had quit because I didn't do "what I was supposed to" on my first attempt at the first workshop in Mexico, I would be further away from my goals. Through this experience I now understand awareness is the first of many tiny steps which moves us into something new. And it is the starting point, not the quitting point.

Another great starting point is checking in with the wisdom of your body. How do you feel? If you feel "off," this is your body letting you know things are out of alignment. This is where you get to choose to do something different or keep feeling worse. And if you are someone who has shut yourself off from feeling or notice you don't really feel anything, this may be your starting point. You have probably heard "what you focus on expands." So, what are you focusing on?

I feel it is vital to mention that you must really listen to the messages your body is giving you. What are you aware of in your body? Pain and discomfort are how your body communicates it is not happy with how you are taking care of it. When those symptoms are ignored, the body continues to deteriorate, and often there are irreversible consequences.

Here are some ways your body may be communicating with you: headaches, inflammation, excess weight, general aches and pains, irritability, and loss of mojo and energy. Do not ignore these!

I have spent the last eighteen years of my life building and acting from my awareness. This practice has helped me dive into the personal and professional areas of my life. I have also aligned with a few besties who are walking this journey with me.

Although I didn't know it at the time, all those action steps around my awareness have brought me to share my story with you. And all of those "right" and "wrong" steps have given me experiences to grow my wisdom and knowledge. These days, I'm able to surrender to my experiences, unpack them, and continue my growth path of living deeper and hiding less. This sometimes takes time and space. And as a teacher, it often feels like there is no extra time or space.

Your time feels limited, but it's imperative that you create time off. Book it! It's important. I know excuses will come up but do it anyway. It can literally be lifesaving.

Often, we do not feel like we are doing enough because we have a perfectionist mindset, or we are always aiming for the ideal. Once we become aware of something, the next moment, our mind says we need to nail that shift in our lives immediately and if we don't, we have failed. And then why would we even try? It's too hard. This thinking is a cyclical rut we can fall into, and it can be very challenging to get out of, especially if those around us don't know what is going on or are in the same rut.

These beginning realizations are the keys to stepping out of the rut or the beliefs which are holding us back. Once we become aware of something, it gives us the power to change it. This change usually happens over time with small steps. Often, these steps are so tiny we do not attribute them to anything, and sometimes we give up because we haven't reached the goal we are working toward in the time frame we have given ourselves.

It is okay to give yourself some grace and shift your timeline.

Are You Aiming for the Ideal and Failing?

Ben Hardy and Dan Sullivan define ideals as follows: "Ideals are like the horizon in the desert. They illuminate the path up ahead and give you direction for setting achievable and measurable targets. But like the horizon, the ideal itself is immeasurable, unreachable, and constantly moving. Ideals are not for measuring yourself against. Why measure yourself against something you can never reach?" (*The Gap and The Gain,* 165).

As I read their book, *The Gap and The Gain*, I began to understand I had an ideal of the many roles I played in my life, and I held those ideals in my conscious and unconscious mind. It showed up as negative self-talk about myself when I was frustrated with my husband. Unconsciously, it also undermined my ability to be unapologetically me because what if I didn't get it "right"?

Upon realizing that the ideals I was aiming for were all false and no one could achieve them, I shifted how I approached the negative thoughts in my brain. I began to toss them out when they showed up in my thinking and my actions. With practice, I slowly realized the negative thoughts were not true. Before, I may not have even noticed I was having them, yet once aware, I consciously chose to release them. This was so powerful for me as I didn't feel the drag of those ideas in my daily life and the amazing things I'm up to. I am a great mom and wife! And I fully believe this shift in beliefs creates more confidence in myself in all areas of my life. It also allows me to model what is real in life and have great conversations both in my head and with other people.

Your Turn
Building Your Awareness

I would like to pause here and bring your attention to the present moment, so you can begin to integrate the shift in your mindset. Grab a journal or something to write on and consider the following questions:

- ✓ What are you now aware of regarding ideals and perfection that you were not aware of before?

- ✓ What patterns or themes do you notice repeatedly showing up in your life?

- ✓ What messages is your body giving you that you may be ignoring?

From the above questions, what are one or two realizations you would like to follow up on with small action steps?

Awareness One:

_____

_____

Action Steps:

_____

_____

Awareness Two:

_____

_____

Action Steps:

_____

_____

Chapter 2

Fueling Your Body to Teach

We live in a society which expects us to be overwhelmed and overstimulated. This leads us to not taking care of ourselves. This feeling leaks into all areas of our lives. Unfortunately, it is the norm. I'd like to propose that the food we eat needs to fuel us for maximum capacity and energy, not just fill our bellies. Regular, healthy sleep cycles aid in bringing fuel as well. We need this to rejuvenate us on all levels so we are better able to show up fully and contribute to the world in our own unique ways. Adding in meditation is the icing on the cake as we step into self-care to create a foundation for the unique impact we are here to have. And the good news is we have control over all the above choices.

Using Real Food to Fuel You

Teachers have many balls in the air on any given day. Eating food which actually fuels the body with energy and focuses the mind is imperative so you can continue to grow your capacity. If you commit to eating foods that fuel you to do your best, it will be worth it. And it often doesn't take more time, it simply requires a bit of planning. Delegating planning time can be a game changer.

I was blessed to grow up with lots of homemade food. One year, on our way home after spending Christmas with my family, I asked my son, "What was one of your favourite parts of the holiday?"

He responded, "THE FOOD! It doesn't matter what it is Mom, it is always amazing!"

When I asked my mom about it, she told me one of the reasons she cooked so much from scratch was my allergy to MSG. This is an example of the silver lining to something as challenging as headaches! Even though I hated having that allergy as a teenager, looking back I'm grateful. I appreciate the value of homemade food, and I'm now a great cook. I understand why my dad wasn't interested in eating in restaurants. The food was never as good as my mom's. The power of having good food to fuel you is priceless.

When my daughter visits houses where she is fed mostly processed food, carbs with fillers, and high sugars, she becomes very impulsive and hyperactive. We had the misfortune of experiencing this impulsivity in the grocery store one memorable occasion.

She asked for anything that caught her attention and was unable to stop the behaviour. This was unusual for her because normally when we shopped, she would suggest a few things and not care too much if they were not bought. When we got back into the car after the second grocery store and the hundredth time of her asking if we could buy something which caught her eye, I spoke to her about it, as I was in tears. My lack of sleep didn't help my emotions! That experience was a huge eye opener for me about the effect of food on our body and mind.

Her response was so telling. She said, "Well, why didn't you just ask me to stop?"

I responded with, "Would you like to discuss how many times I asked you to stop?"

I could see the realization hit her from the look in her eyes. She got it, and no other words were needed.

Real food versus filler is one of my big takeaways in learning about my body and how it interacts with what I feed it. As a kid, it was always a novelty to have something from a box or package (aka processed), because my mom always cooked from scratch, and so did both of my grandmas.

Now I understand that processed food, which may be convenient to grab and go, doesn't give me the energy I need to do my day well. Possibly more importantly, processed food taxes my digestive system and uses up more energy to digest, which leaves me with less energy for what I love to do. The heightened state it creates in my nervous system is also alarming, leaving me never wanting my children to have processed sugar or other stimulants. And I know completely avoiding processed food is not realistic in today's world. So, I do my best to discourage it and educate them and let them choose… most of the time.

I don't think we really grasp the impact the food we eat has on our bodies and in our lives. I have experienced this process in my own life and the impact on the behaviour and experience of my own children. I feel it is a significant message to share with others. I do not want to give away energy to have to digest crap food which doesn't fuel me. It actually leaves me craving more and eating more empty calories, thus gaining weight and creating inflammation, all while sucking my energy. No thanks!

I was surprised at the little adjustments I could make around food, which shifted how I felt and gave me more energy in my day. And I do not eat 100 percent healthy all the time. (Iced cappuccinos are one of my weaknesses.)

Eating my biggest meal at lunchtime gives me the energy to succeed in my day and not have an afternoon crash, which I used to fix with dark chocolate. It also has me eating a lighter dinner rather than stuffing myself because I'm starving. This leads me to sleeping better and not feeling so full and uncomfortable.

And rather than snacking all afternoon, adding hot water to my day, by using a thermos cup in my classroom, kept me hydrated and my brain firing more effectively. It also cut down on my sugar intake and extra calories that were not needed.

As an adult, I have continued to enjoy cooking great food. I learned and added to the knowledge and experience through yoga and Ayurveda. I began to realize good food wasn't the only thing which could make me feel better.

Over the past six to seven years, I've learned, implemented, and now teach others how to fuel their body with real food and daily practices which you can apply on your own and do not cost extra. In fact, fueling my body more intentionally often saves me money as I'm more deliberate in my choices and spend less on filler foods and emotional buying. Here are some ideas to begin to implement.

- Eat your biggest meal at lunchtime with high fat and protein to sustain your energy.

- Drink warm or hot water between meals to hydrate your body and have your neurons firing optimally.

- Eat dinner by 6 p.m. so your body can digest your food before you go to bed.

- Eat more whole foods to ensure your body is not using extra energy to digest processed sugar and carbs.

- Buy what appeals to you in the fresh section of your grocery store.

- Create meal plans with your family so you're not in decision fatigue when you go to prepare dinner.

- Keep in mind the long game for how you want your body to feel instead of the short quick fix.

Your Turn
What Are You Ready to Shift?

Take a moment and reflect on what you have just read. What is one thing you would like to shift around the food you are currently eating? Here are a few questions to get you thinking about simple shifts:

✓ When do you eat?

✓ What food are you fueling yourself with?

✓ What are you doing while you are eating?

✓ How do you prepare your food?

✓ Who are you eating with?

And remember to give yourself permission to take one small step at a time instead of thinking you must shift it all at once. Also, give yourself some grace for not getting it right all the time. Fueling the body is an ever-changing practice which will shift with the seasons.

The Power of Sleep and Rest–The Forgotten Fuel

Sleep has the power to shift how we feel. We get the opportunity to top up our capacity daily. However, there are many factors which influence the quality of our rest. Past experiences, what we eat, who we spend time with, what we do in our days, our stress levels, and when and where we sleep all play a role in the quantity and quality of our rest time. Our overall health is dependent on our sleep quality. By tapping into the power of sleep, teachers can live their lives to the fullest without being depleted.

During my greatest health challenges, I was hot all the time, had headaches almost daily, and slept any chance I could, sometimes more than sixteen hours. My energy was often low, especially when I wasn't on the go. My life consisted of working three jobs and hanging out with my friends.

This was also the time when I came across a chakra workshop. The lady who taught it was an iridologist. This pivotal moment changed the trajectory of my health. After the seminar, I went for a session with her, and she gave me a plan to help me with my overheating, headaches, and energy levels, and I followed it to a T.

Why wouldn't I? I was so tired of being tired, and none of the medical professionals I saw had any solutions. After the first week of following through with what the iridologist told me, I was no longer hot all the time. That result was enough to have me continue to follow her suggestions. Looking back, I believe my body was on its way to having a chronic sleep issue. I'm so grateful for her wisdom and the choice to shift my habits and lifestyle.

Ten years ago, before I was introduced to Ayurveda, I used to take three-hour naps on weekends due to my exhaustion. These naps left me with less time to spend with my own kiddos and husband.

We all know sleep is essential. For me it is *the* keystone habit—the one which holds it all together. If I have more than two nights of going to bed late, I spiral down. In self-discovery, here is how my downfall goes:

- I get cranky with those around me.

- I have no patience.

- I doubt myself.

- I lose motivation to do what I love to do.

- I hide in games, books, and movies.

- I have no desire to cook.

- I eat processed foods high in sugars and carbs.

- I don't reach out to my friends.

- I don't tidy up after myself.

- I get angry at my choices.

- I blame others around me.

Lack of sleep has me doing all the things which make me feel awful. I used to have so many excuses as to why I couldn't go to bed early. Now I understand if I choose to get on top of my sleep and make it the most important part of my day by beginning to wind down at 8 p.m., I'm golden! If I allow others to influence my decisions, ignore my own commitments, or avoid my inner wisdom, I don't get the sleep I need.

What do you believe about your schedule and sleep? Is it possible some of your beliefs need to shift so you can feel well-rested? How can you begin to communicate with those around you so you can get the sleep you need to be the best you possible and show up fully for what you are meant to offer this world?

Where Do You Fit?

As humans and teachers, we do a lot in a day. There are hundreds, if not thousands, of stimulants which have us multitasking throughout our waking hours and even some while we attempt to sleep. For lots of us, we hold down two full-time jobs: professsionally and personally with family. And then we lay down in bed and expect our body and mind to just stop.

As you have probably discovered, your mind struggles to shut off, and when it does, it often starts up again, sometimes waking you up at 3 a.m. Or you are doing tasks late at night because this is when you feel you have time for yourself. You may also experience the go-go adrenalin rush you get from the constant stimulation. And this hit has you doing more when what you really need is to slow down, allow yourself a pause, and create some space.

This is where your beliefs might have you saying, "I can't, I have too much to do."

Take a breath and take a moment right now. Close your eyes and take five breaths... and then maybe another five. Notice what happens to your body when you give it a moment to breathe. And it took less than thirty seconds.

You matter! Yes, you do have time for yourself! The hard reality is, if you don't start to carve out time for yourself right now, your body is going to force you to by getting sick with the cold, or flu, or something worse. Listen to the little messages it is giving you before they get bigger and turn into something irreversible. Begin to make sleep and rest a priority. It will change your life and the lives of those closest to you.

A few things to consider as you dissect your sleep.

- What stimulants are you ingesting? (Caffeine, sugar, alcohol, spicy foods?)

- What is your stress level? What do you do daily to decrease the stress you carry?

- When do you have down time? This may be a few minutes to yourself where you stop and take time just for you?

- What does your screen time look like during your day, including what you do in your classroom?

- When do you turn your devices/screens off at night?

- How do you decompress, digest, and assimilate your day?

Your Turn
Get a Better Sleep

Give yourself time to wind down before bed. Since we have lots on our schedule, decide what time you would like to be in bed. I would suggest before ten so you can hit the optimal sleep and rejuvenation time between 10 p.m. and 2 a.m. Plan your evening so you have ten to thirty minutes to wind yourself down. I'm often doing this with my youngest, which means more quality time with her. This also has me going to bed most nights before 9 p.m., which is amazing because then I'm up around 5 a.m. when no one else is. This is my favourite time of the day, as it is so peaceful and calm.

If I'm not beginning to wind down by 8:30, I get my second wind and then can't go to sleep.

Now the question is, what is your wind-down routine? If you think about it from a physical standpoint, your body has gone through a lot in one day. Going for a short walk or running outside is a favourite at different times of the year. Sometimes this includes stargazing. Stretching is another simple go-to you can do anywhere. Yoga or ball rolling creates full-body awareness and stretching, which allows the body to begin to unwind some of what it has stored from the day. Creating and implementing this wind down takes some of the mind chatter and body stimulation away so your body can fully relax and rest deeply.

From a mental perspective, winding the mind down can be done in several ways. Experiment and find what works best for you, as it isn't a one-size-fits-all. Here are a few suggestions:

    ✓ Journaling—have a journal and pencil beside your bed, write three wins for today, three wins you hope to get for tomorrow, and gratitude for the day.

    ✓ Brain Dump—write whatever comes up. Sometimes it might be your thoughts, and other times it can be a to-do list.

Our body and mind are interesting and interconnected. One person never operates exactly like another, which totally makes sense as we are all unique and have different experiences.

Know this is a process. You may notice things in the first few days you begin shifting your routines and habits, or it may take a while. I have been practicing these habits for more than seven years, and I still notice shifts. I also fall off the wagon and forget or get out of the routine of winding down in the evening. Know that you don't have to get it right; it is a practice.

Get curious about what works for you. If you have spent years struggling with sleep, it may take months to get it into alignment. Keep taking the action steps and be aware of the other stressors in your life which may be playing a role in disrupting your sleep. Give yourself the grace you would give a friend. Be kind to yourself.

Meditation Quiets the Mind and Relaxes the Body

Meditation can be like the caffeine pick-me-up you look for after lunch during your school day. However, it doesn't have the same side effects. Sometimes your gas tank runs out before you are ready to sleep again; this is where the idea that rest can be 10X'd through meditation comes in. Use meditation to give your mind, body, emotions, and mental capacity a rest so you can pick up and continue on more effectively in your day.

I had a lightbulb moment with meditation! One day, I came home from school and sat in my husband's recliner. I had no energy left, and I still needed to be mom for the evening, which meant cooking dinner, interacting with my family, and preparing for my next day of teaching.

I hit play on a ten-minute meditation and set an alarm in case I fell asleep. I chose ten minutes because that was the time I had before I needed to begin dinner. For me, cooking dinner is a sacred piece of being a mom as I show my love through my food.

After those ten minutes, I opened my eyes, totally amazed as I felt like a brand-new person! My mind was clear, and I had the energy I needed to get up and hang out with those I love and be fully present. This was an aha moment for me of the power of meditation. And still, I struggle to do it regularly!

Mindfulness and Meditation
Life Practices

Do you believe meditation must be done sitting, not moving, and with nothing going on in your mind? This is a false belief that can sometimes deter you from using meditation for rest as you feel you can't sit quietly with your mind silent.

The words *meditation* and *mindfulness* seem to be interchangeable these days. For me, mindfulness is paying attention to what I'm currently working on as opposed to working mindlessly and thinking of something else. I notice I am less mindful when I'm stressed. I am most mindful when I'm cooking, walking, or connecting with family and friends. Often people express that their mindfulness is like meditation, and it rejuvenates them.

Formal meditation practice may have a bit more structure to it, but not always. I feel like I should let you know I am a bit of a rebel, and thus I forgo lots of the "rules" for this introspection time. Meditation can be like a three-hour nap rolled into fifteen minutes. Sometimes I sit or lie down and listen to a guided practice, other times I lie on the floor while focusing on my breath. Whatever you choose for your meditation, it's helpful to choose a specific time and place you can practice daily. This has your body and mind beginning to set up even before you begin. When I was breast-feeding one of my children, I used it as an initiator to sit quietly and breathe. This benefited both of us.

Kaizen is a concept which was introduced to me several years ago, and I hear it often now. It means 1 percent continuous improvement over time. And if you apply it over a year, you get 37 percent better. I love applying this concept to meditation and mindfulness. Sometimes my 1 percent looks like stopping and taking ten breaths because I don't have time to meditate. My classroom was in the basement of the school, and I used the stairs as a reminder to slow down and breathe. This was a great prompt as teachers are often on the go, and the simple reminder to slow down was powerful.

Where can you fit mindfulness and/or meditation into your life? Let me ask you again: Where do you want to make time to fit meditation into your day, so you feel like you have been gifted a three-hour nap? It is so important to set a time and then begin to follow through so this practice happens and can be automated. If you do not, this habit will fall to the side, and other seemingly more urgent things will pop up and take over. I'm going to guess you are already experiencing this with some of your current self-care practices. They get pushed to the bottom of the list because "urgent" things arise and take precedence. Give yourself permission to pause and take those two to ten minutes to implement meditation into your day. I know it doesn't seem like it will make a difference, but for me, it still makes a huge difference! And giving students time to practice it in your room will multiply the ripple effect in your classroom. Mindfulness supports our nervous system because it allows us to be in this moment, not worrying about what is next or tomorrow.

Your Turn
Take Your Time to Create

Get out your phone and set an alarm. I suggest setting it for three minutes after the recess or lunch bell has rung and your students have left the room. When your alarm goes off, set a two-minute timer. Pause whatever you are doing, close your eyes, and breathe for those two minutes. Alternatively, you can put on a guided meditation.

Chapter 3

Burnout Happens Without Clear Boundaries

Your ability to say yes or no to something or someone may be leading you directly to exhaustion and possibly burnout. The road to burnout is not labelled. We often feel we are "fine," living day-to-day and don't even realize it is happening. And because lots of those around us also feel burned out we do not realize it is detrimental to our health or that there is a different way. Where do you sit regarding your own fatigue and burnout? Take a moment to reflect on this, you may even want to pull out your journal and do a brain dump.

Boundaries

What you say yes and no to for yourself defines your boundaries and shows others how to treat you. It can also keep burnout from happening. If you are the one they can count on, you will always be asked. Getting clear on your own values and plans will support you in staying aligned and communicating your boundaries. Asking for support for yourself is imperative. Ask for what you need and keep asking until you find the right person who can support you. And you may have to say no several times to the same request before others get that you are not available to help.

The vibrancy and connection I found in the leadership community across Canada when I said yes to Halifax and the Canadian Student Leadership Conference was infectious. It lit me up about teaching again. I absolutely loved the people I met, both students and teachers. This new focus and enthusiasm kept me teaching a few more years. However, I spread myself too thin because I didn't create better boundaries. Looking back, this was the beginning of my road to burnout.

I began to say yes to things in my school which added more to my plate and took away from my classroom time. The planning and teaching of high school leadership became a bit of a monster as there were so many cool opportunities to say yes to. And I wanted to do it all! Another was helping plan the Alberta Student Leadership Conference in Airdrie. Because I was struggling with my boundaries, these extra amazing tasks taxed me too much over time.

Looking back, had I created greater or firmer boundaries, perhaps I would still be teaching in a classroom. One of the things I find most debilitating about the teaching profession is that if you are great at something, even if it wears you down, people see you as handling it, and you don't necessarily get the support you need to keep your vibrancy up beyond the just-barely-surviving mode. This is where asking for what you need comes in. I didn't ask for help as often as I needed it. I found myself looking at other teachers and classes, noticing their struggle, and thinking it was worse than mine and they needed the help instead of me.

The combination of having a challenging class, being pulled in many directions because I said yes to so many other great opportunities, and my drive to support others, including other teachers in my school, my friends, and family, caused me to hit a wall. What fascinated me is the people around me could see I was in burnout. When I began to dissect this burnout, more than a year after it happened (because it took me that long to see it as burnout), I realized some of the people around me attempted to help and tell me to take a break. Their comments triggered me! It brought out the "I'm strong, I can do this" part of me. The "don't give up, just push through for the next three months."

Looking back, I wish I had taken their advice.

Once my body decided it was finished, I ignored the signs. The stubborn voice of "I'm strong enough to do this, these kids need me, and who will be able to handle them?" came up very loud. And still, I pushed through with a chest infection, the flu, and a possible blood clot in my leg. My body attempted to tell me I was in burnout for four weeks straight. And I pushed through as I needed to prove to those who didn't think I could do it that I could. (And maybe this was more for me than them.)

As a teacher, you may find yourself saying yes to so many requests it sends you into overload regularly. These requests can come from students, colleagues, the administration, and your own friends and family. And sometimes all at the same time. With our technology today, a student can be asking a question as they stand next to you, your family can be texting you about evening plans, a colleague can be at your door, and an email from parents and administration can be arriving in your inbox each with its own request, all at the same time. Knowing the demands of your job and that it is okay to say no will support you in weeding out what you want to say no to and where you truly want to invest your time and energy.

Often you may find yourself saying yes to invitations which come from your administration or team to impress them and be a good team player, or just because you have been taught to say yes to those in charge. You may be a people pleaser and say yes to everything you are asked. Remember you get to decide what experiences you choose to have.

If you began saying no to three requests each day, what would you do with the time and space created?

I'd also like to invite you to stop saying yes to please other people and start saying yes to what you love and what brings you joy. Though it may seem selfish to say no and focus on self, it's actually extremely healthy to create boundaries and then stand firm in them. Many who have ignored self for a long time end up in the same place I did: burned out. Remember, YOU are the most essential asset you have. If you want to be fully available to show up and bring your best, you need to start doing more things just for you. And YES, those around you will begin to step up and take some of the load— even your children. You can delegate and then *not* do it yourself when they don't follow through on the first time or redo it because they didn't do it how you would. In some areas someone else may pick the task up without even being asked because no one else is taking responsibility for it. This new routine will probably take a bit of time to settle in, so add in some grace for everyone, including yourself.

You may also need to drop the belief you need to do it all yourself, like I did.

Your Turn
Decide What to Say Yes To

Let's pause here again and take a few deep breaths. What you have just read on burnout may have triggered you. You may now realize you might be in burnout, and that is okay. The imperative next step is to reach out. If you are feeling you can begin to navigate this on your own, here are some journal questions to spend some time on. However, if you are feeling overwhelmed and emotional about where you are, reach out and ask for help or have a conversation with someone you trust.

✓ Here are some journal questions to support you around shifting how you spend your time:

- What do YOU want to do with your time?
- What do you desire to feel as you navigate your day?
- What impact or ripple effect do you want to have in this world?
- Are you currently having your desired ripple effect in most areas of your life?
- What is getting in your way?
- Who do you need to communicate with to begin to shift to be more in alignment with what you want?

I find the Five-Word Exercise to be helpful to create indicators of what you want to say yes or no to. Give yourself ten to fifteen minutes and possibly invite a colleague to do it as well.

✓ Five-Word Exercise:

- Pull out your journal or a piece of paper.
- Start with a quick brain dump about how you currently feel. Are you feeling overwhelmed, rushed, happy, organized, exhausted, or behind? Write down whatever words come up as you contemplate this. Don't censor it.
- Next, sit back and take a few breaths and imagine what an amazing day would feel like.
- What would create more space for you and your students?
- What do you really want to feel as you navigate your day?

- List the adjectives you *want* to feel and experience throughout your day.

Once you have completed this list, choose your top five. Post this list somewhere in your room where you will see it regularly and use it as a quick reference and a guide for what you say yes or no to. If it doesn't align with any of those five words, it's probably something you can say no to.

A friend once told me, "I'm not responsible for someone else's disappointment." So, when you say no to something, it is absolutely 110 percent okay if it disappoints someone else, especially if it didn't align with you and what you are up to.

You may want to do this exercise in your home with your family and those you live with, as well as with the students in your classroom. However, start by doing it yourself so you are clear on what you desire.

What Is Your Current Relationship with Burnout?

Being in burnout or heading in that direction often makes it challenging to see you are in the middle of it. It is a bit like the frog in water before you bring it to a boil. As you gradually get busier and busier you don't notice how depleted and dysfunctional you get when it is your day-to-day. And then suddenly you realize you are drowning and are not sure how it happened. Or how to get out of it.

I went for a walk and visited with a teacher friend and was saddened to hear she felt nonfunctional in her days and was barely holding it together. A close relative had passed away earlier in the year. She had spent her February break saying goodbye to him and her April break spending time with family and working through her own grief as she navigated the funeral. And then she went back to work on Monday.

What breaks my heart about this situation is often teachers feel they need to push through and continue after a stressful or traumatic event in their lives. The time it takes to heal from grief is not a weekend. It may take months or years. Taking some time off for yourself can be challenging, but it is essential. Teachers often don't take needed time off because they perceive all the extra work is not worth it: lesson planning, setting students up for success with a different teacher, and possibly dreading what they will return to.

It is also challenging to hand the class over to someone else, no matter how qualified that individual is, because we know the stress it can cause some of the students. In some situations, extensive planning may be required. However, all the teachers who I know who have had the courage to take time to heal and recuperate have said it was the best thing they could have done for both themselves and their families.

On the other hand, there will be occasions when you just need extra time to deal with life situations for yourself, other family members, or even close friends, which is completely okay. Providing yourself this gift will give you a clear head and the energy to take care of your personal life without having your professional workload looming over your head. Short term leave is there for a reason. Do not be afraid to use it.

You are the one who chooses where you invest your time. It isn't always an easy decision. Get in the habit of saying no when you don't have the space in your calendar. Someone else will say yes to the request. And if enough people say no, the administration will realize more people power is needed, which might even begin to change the face of education.

We all know that occasionally things overlap like planning a concert and writing report cards and at the same time having a special guest show at your school. It is important to have your year plan on your wall, in front of you, so all you need to do is glance at it and know what is going on.

Giving yourself a day at the beginning of each month to look at the next three to six months is so powerful for planning. It helps you stay aware of everything going on and may help in protecting time for yourself, in keeping your students aware of what's on the horizon, and it could inspire you to be the voice of reason in the meeting who says, "Hey, there are three other events going on at the same time. Adding this will be too much." Be the voice of reason in the room, even if you get funny looks!

Another strategy is to ask yourself the question: Does this align with my own goals right now? If the answer is yes, next ask yourself, "Do I have the capacity to take this on?" And last, ask, "Do I have the space in my calendar to fully commit to this?" If any of your answers are no, then decline the request.

For the longest time, I kind of set goals, and sometimes I wrote them down, but I really didn't focus on them. I had been taught about goals more than once, but none of the strategies really stuck with me. I realized I needed the process of dreaming big, working with others, and then breaking it down into small action steps. And most importantly, devising a schedule in my calendar to make it all happen while remembering that I do not need to get it right.

Through the Master of You workshop which I participate in three times per year and run my own version of, I have intentional goals and the action steps I can take to bring my dreams into reality. Like everything else in life, this is a trajectory and a process. Sometimes I'm right on track, and other times I need to change things up as the goal has changed or my timeline has shifted. However, doing these processes several times a year keeps me moving forward in whatever I want to focus on both personally and professionally. It makes sure I don't get lost in the day-to-day happenings. I believe you get to be the driver in your life! But you need to step forward and claim the driver's seat and then have the courage to step on the gas.

Possible Signs You Might Be Heading to Burnout

Whether you feel you are in burnout or on your way there, you can shift it. And a heads up, this might feel like ripping a Band-Aid off if you are unaware of how depleted you are or avoiding getting real about it. I encourage you to reach out to me, a good friend, or even a paid professional if this feels like a kick in the teeth.

It took me a year to realize I was in burnout mode after I stepped away from my classroom. And another year to unpack the effect it had on me. There is no shame in burnout. Being burned out means you got lost somewhere in it all and were not sure of the way back.

Now we have brought your awareness to where you are and have given you some simple tools to fuel yourself. I'd like to touch base on where you are at with burnout.

You might be in burnout if you find yourself:

- Saying it's all good… I'm surviving.

- Not sleeping and exhausted.

- Not wanting to get out of bed.

- Gaining or losing weight.

- Unable to meet the regular demands of life.

- Losing interest and motivation for things you used to love to do.

- Experiencing reduced productivity.

- Feeling helpless.

- Feeling hopeless.

- Feeling resentful.

- Feeling cynical.

- Experiencing frequent headaches or muscle pain.

- Getting sick frequently.

- Having a sense of self-doubt.

- Feeling isolated and alone.

- Turning to alcohol, food, or drugs to function.

- Constantly feeling anxious.

Even now when I look at this list, I say to myself, "maybe I wasn't burned out." And then I read some more of the list, and I can check lots of them off.

What do you do if you are feeling like you might be burned out or heading in that direction? Talk to someone. I do not feel it is okay to be exhausted all the time. There are things you can do to support yourself. Speak to your admin, take a few days off and take some time for yourself, book an appointment with your doctor, or talk to a life coach. Find someone you can be real with; don't sugar coat it. You might also want to take a trusted friend to an appointment so they can help you unpack what was said later. Don't just ignore burnout like I did.

Chapter 4

The Crossover Between Home and School

Balance between home life and the classroom is an ever-changing concept we often attempt to stabilize without a solid plan or team to support us. Thus, we seem to push through too often. Finding the equilibrium of leaving schoolwork at school is possible, and it depends on the time of year and what is going on both at home and at school. Viewing your family as a formal team and regular planning can help you create systems which support you and your family, especially during those busy times. Choosing to push through is an old belief system which depletes you even more for your long game and takes away the fulfillment and joy of teaching and time spent with others.

Stop Pushing Through

I hear so many teachers talk about pushing through. "I just have to push through a few more weeks until February break, and then I can take some time for me." And then they get sick because their body didn't have the capacity to push through. When we force ourselves to *push through* we are ignoring the body's biological signs that we need a break. The compounded stress of feeling we need to continue when our body says stop has our systems shutting down as they are already on overload. This unhealthy response creates even more stress.

This overextension of ourselves often shows up before we have time off as we feel we can push through until the break. It's like we can see the light at the end of the tunnel, so we put our head down and forge forward, ignoring our body signals even more. When I push through, I find myself even more depleted, and I'm not able to take the week off and recover enough to be recharged again. I'm still draggy and uninspired. Overextending ourselves does not work! It led me to exhaustion then burnout.

Where is it leading you? You matter! Give yourself permission to stop pushing through; take a few days and regroup. If you can't take time off from school, clear your schedule by letting people know you are not available. Also, ask for help on the basics like cooking, cleaning, and parenting. I have had conversations with parents who feel guilty for asking someone else to take their children for a couple of hours or even overnight. If your children are anything like mine, they are super excited to hang out with someone else. And the other people love spending time with your children! It is a win-win. Don't create stories in your head that it makes you a bad parent. It is not true. Ask for help; we are not meant to travel this journey solo.

In the summer of 2013, I found out I was pregnant—a big surprise as we thought we had finished having children. We already had an eight-year-old son and an eighteen-month-old daughter. As I was considered high risk due to being the ripe old age of thirty-six, my health care providers insisted on doing some early ultrasounds.

I have a very positive outlook on life. You would say I'm on the optimistic side. Thus, having ultrasounds wasn't a big deal, and I believed it would all turn out fine. The first appointment was the beginning of an emotional roller coaster for me and my family.

After the first ultrasound, they sent me for another one, which was more detailed. In the second ultrasound, we found out my pregnancy was fatal. Our daughter was not expected to live because her heart and brain were not forming correctly.

This situation was heartbreaking and overwhelming. Being the strong person I am, the next day I went back to work as if nothing had changed. Luckily, one of the teaching assistants in the school knew something was up, so she asked me if I was okay. This was the question I needed to be asked. It cracked the fragile framework of all the emotions I had bottled up inside and hadn't allowed myself to feel at the beginning of this trauma.

I pulled her into the bathroom and shared that my baby would not make it. She was so supportive. I didn't know she'd had a similar experience. She insisted I go and speak to my administration right away, as it was recess. I went from being someone holding it all together to falling apart as I told my principal what was going on. I went home by lunch. It is interesting how I felt the need to show up in my classroom even though I had a traumatic experience going on. When I look back, I have no idea how I thought I was supposed to go to school and teach, I just did it. My autopilot seemed to have taken over.

Support

Those around you are your rocks. They are essential for your success. Intentionally choose them and then show up fully to be supported and to support them.

The first time I saw psychologist and author Dr. Jody Carrington live, I realized I had isolated myself and I wasn't truly showing up to be fully supported. I remember feeling my lowest and having the courage to send a message to my women's group to tell them I was a mess; the tears were flowing, and I was thinking I had no one who I could reach out to who would understand. As soon as I sent the message, I felt better. It was that day I dropped the belief I had of, "I don't have any close friends, I have no one to reach out to." I chose to begin to step out of being a victim and step into owning my life and my choices.

With an exhale, the next promise I made myself was to talk to my husband and let him know how I was truly doing, instead of pretending I was good. The details are not clear as to the conversation or the message. I just know it was the point where I started to be real about how hard things felt and what I was struggling with. It was a tipping point for me. I no longer had to have the conversations which were going on in my head with just myself. Others knew how I was really doing. They may not have been able to understand it all, but they listened, gave me hugs, and let me know I wasn't alone. They were there for me no matter what.

This seemingly small action of sending a text shifted things for me, and I no longer felt desperately alone. Especially since the reality was that I had amazing people around me, I just had to reach out. I still use this strategy when I'm feeling low, and I also use it for others. When I'm feeling great or want to reach out because someone has popped into my head, I send them a message. Sometimes it is just a simple emoji. It lets them know they are not alone. I'm also not attached to their response. In return, those who do respond with a "How did you know?" or "I needed to hear that today, thank you," light me up and remind me to continue to reach out as it lifts others up.

The more I'm supported, the stronger I am! When I choose not to carry my burdens alone, they do not crush me bit by bit without my being aware of it. I have a shoulder or two, often more, to lean on, and this also gives me another perspective to help me shift my thinking and my situation to move forward and be more aware. I know for me, life's ups and downs are so much easier when I feel confident and supported in what I'm doing, when I know and trust my team has my back.

You will encounter some people with whom you share who do not give you what you need. This may even include your partner. Find someone else to be your confidant in that area. Our partners do not need to be our everything. Some jobs they are not good at, yet some they rock. Don't expect them to be amazing at what they are not good at. Seek out someone who has the capacity to listen and be a shoulder. You may find they need you in a similar way as well. And it might not be another teacher. The intent of these conversations is to make you feel better and shift the energy, not get you stuck in the negative.

Who is your team? Let them know, begin to be more real about what is going on. It might be easier to start these conversations bit by bit to build capacity if it isn't something you are used to. It takes courage to begin to have these chats. They will more than likely be uncomfortable. And it takes endurance to continue to have them because you know they are awkward. I know you have the grit to do this because you show up in your classroom each day.

Your Turn
Who Is Your Support Team?

Make a list of your support team.

✓ Who do you call, text, or visit on those tough days?

✓ When was the last time you reached out and connected with them?

✓ Would it be helpful for you to do so this week?

If you would like to dive a bit deeper, do some writing about who is good at what. This has you brainstorming those who may have the specific skill set for what you might need in terms of support.

The Planning–Set Yourself Up for Success

If you don't make your own plan, you are part of someone else's. Set aside some time to create your plan. The idea of B minus will support you in continuing to step into this practice as you navigate it over the year. Aiming for the B minus will help you stay out of the rut of perfection which occurs when we always shoot for the A plus. Again, it is a practice; you do not need to get it right all the time. And it is a year-to-year practice, as we continue to hone our planning. When I accomplish my planning on the first Monday of the month, it takes a weight off my shoulders. And the agenda doesn't always roll out how I expect it to, which is okay. Give yourself grace and flexibility as we all know life happens and plans change.

Make time for your planning. Set aside at least sixty to ninety minutes for this.

Here are some questions to consider before you pull your plan together:

- What is your peak time? When do you function the best and have the most creativity? This is the time when you want to schedule your planning.

- How much time do you feel you need before and after school to do what needs to be done? What do you consider a balance when it comes to where you spend your time? (Home, friends, partner, kids, just-for-fun, and extra personal time spent on schoolwork?) And balance doesn't need to mean *equal* in this situation.

- What is your unique formula for balance? This will change throughout the year.

As you consider these questions, be reminded of your role as a teacher. Are you giving too much time to your classroom and students and not enough to yourself and your family?

Look at your boundaries. Who and where are you choosing to invest your time? It is good to say no to the things you don't want to do. Feeling obligated is a big red flag to some of the things you might want to begin to say no to.

Again, it's okay to start with small things. What brings you joy and laughter, what fulfills you? Say yes to those things as they support the balance of bringing in more ease and less stress.

Do you use a digital calendar or a paper one? This can be a bit of a process to begin with, especially if you haven't already shifted to a digital one. It only took me about a year to figure out what worked best for me. And now it saves me so much time. I have a large paper wall calendar in my office for business planning and the week to week on my digital calendar which I can access on my phone or my computer. On the first Monday of each month, I set aside time to work on my calendar. I look at the next three to six months of my life.

Some of the things I consider:

- What can I batch task?

- Who can I delegate to?

- Who can I ask for help?

At a conference, I once heard, he who does the most work, learns the most. Where can you delegate and ask for support from your students to increase their learning and life experience rather than doing all the background prep?

Remember, beyond the curriculum are the front-end skills students need in life. Are you taking away essential life lessons by not allowing them to be more involved in the planning, organization, and creative end of lessons?

Pick one night you can set aside some time to tackle an hour or so for work. Let others in your house know this is your plan. Have someone else take responsibility for dinner that night, including the cleanup. If you have kids, you may even want to ask them to go to the park or do something out of the house, so you have uninterrupted time. Then pull out your schoolwork, plan what must be done, and work on it. DO NOT clean your house or do other odd jobs.

For those of you who are ready to dive deep into this and want more than the above practice to start with, organization, planning, and accountability are where you want to begin.

Your Turn
Plan Your Life!
Create Your Own Schedule, Use Your Calendar

As you begin to look at your calendar once a month, plan your fun time first!

✓ What weekends do you want totally off from school?

✓ Who will you spend your off time with?

✓ What do you want to do, just for fun, alone or with others?

- ✓ What family events would you like to be a part of?

- ✓ What community events are going on that you would like to attend or send your family to while you stay home?

- ✓ What is your significant other's schedule?

- ✓ When can you plan fun activities together?

- ✓ When can you plan for your own personal time or theirs?

- ✓ What is your children's schedule? Bring them into the planning process. It may add an extra layer of complexity, but you are building their life skills.

- ✓ What days do they have off school?

- ✓ What is the schedule of their extra-curricular activities?

- ✓ What events do they want to attend?

Family Meetings

Plan a weekly or monthly family meeting where everyone is present. We do ours on the weekend during a mealtime. This is your life, so plan it out how you want it. Do not leave it to chance or allow someone else to be the driver! Your meeting can be a casual or a more formal process. And they will evolve over time. You can start with these questions: What is working in our house? What is not working? If you want to make it more formal, you can come up with some family values to help guide the household.

Other Time Commitments

Workshops can be a way of sharpening your time-tested skills or learning new ones. They can serve to not only help your performance and morale in the classroom, but also keep you up to date with your Teacher Professional Growth Plan. Keep in mind, personal workshops can also help with all aspects of your life, but they must be carefully worked into your calendars so that you are feeling excited to attend instead of overwhelmed because you didn't organize well.

Personal care like massages, chiropractor, doctor, and dentist must also be maintained. Remember, lots of these are covered by your benefits... use them! It is okay to schedule these in your life to support yourself in feeling better before you hit crisis mode. And in one phone call, email, or conversation you can schedule these appointments for the next three to six months.

Sub Coverage

Do any of the above days in your planning need a sub to be booked? Reach out to your favourite sub and book them now.

The Effect of Using Regular Planning as Tool

This planning and organization process calms my nervous system as I'm not feeling rushed or short on time as often. I also feel like I have a handle on what is going on in my life. What does arise without notice can be taken care of because I'm not feeling overwhelmed or anxious about the rest of my schedule. It is a relief when I book my massages ahead of time as then they seem to arrive at just the right time. I don't wait for three months and then realize how stiff and sore I am.

I can say no to people because I know I have something scheduled or my calendar already feels full enough. It gives me a guide as to where I'm investing my time. This was a huge game changer for me. My anxiety shows up when I'm overscheduled. Now I rarely have too much on my plate because I don't like it when my anxiety takes over. I now realize I can prevent it.

As I mentioned earlier, you can be the driver of your life. Yes, I know you have commitments, families, friends, and other things all vying for your time. But ultimately you are the one who decides. And again, I know I may be challenging some of your beliefs and assumptions. Nothing will change if you do not question your life and think critically about what you would like to change and what is working well.

This setting up of your life puts you in the decision seat. You can create boundaries and set an example for those around you.

Here are some additional tips for planning and organizing your life:

- Use a calendar or planner to keep track of your appointments and deadlines.
- Create a system for organizing your electronic files and documents and then use it.
- Delegate tasks to others when possible.
- Take breaks throughout the day to avoid burnout.
- Make time for yourself to relax and recharge.
- Be mindful of your time and how you spend it.

Organizing your life can be a challenge, but it is worth it. By taking the time to plan and prioritize, you can reduce stress, increase productivity, and improve your overall well-being. It is also important to teach it to your own children.

This setting up of your life puts you in the decision-making seat. You can create boundaries and set an example for those around you. Do you want your own children or those who are around you to learn overwhelm and putting others first as the norm? What are you modeling for all those who are watching?

It is always interesting to me when I say no to helping someone and they usually find someone else to do the job. This is great life problem-solving for those around you and a learning opportunity for them. When you are always the go-to, they do not build the critical thinking and problem-solving skills they need to function on their own or to create a larger team of support. And yes, it is hard to watch them struggle and fail, but failing is an essential skill to learn because then they pick up, put themselves back together, and move on. They do this while knowing you have their back and will support them, but they also know you don't need to do it for them.

Being someone's go-to person can be exhausting, and if you know you cannot fully commit because of your own boundaries, it is necessary to decline. I find this interesting to watch. First, they must resource and find someone else, which is a great problem-solving skill that must be honed. Next, yes, they may struggle—and that can be hard to watch—but it requires they dig a little deeper. And last, it absolutely may end in failure, and failing is an essential part of life. They will learn to pick themselves up and put themselves back together to move on. You are still a part of that person's support team, but you are modeling boundaries that they are also seeing.

Leaving School at School

Creating a separation between school and home is a powerful practice. I use the word *practice* because it is something we need to work on regularly, assessing and reassessing depending on the time of the year and what is going on at home and at school. For some of you who have been doing this for years, this will challenge your beliefs. Others will sigh with relief because you have been struggling with it. And some of you will already have this figured out. If this feels challenging for you, begin with small steps.

Not taking work home was always a challenge for me. After I finished teaching, I would tidy up my space and decide what was on my must-do list before the next morning, put it in my bag, and head home. Some days, I was so done I didn't tidy up; I just grabbed whatever was right in front of me, stuffed it in my bag, and headed out the door. Once I got home, I would drop my bag in the back porch and spend my evening with my family. Often, I didn't touch the work I had brought home, and usually, it was on my mind, weighing me down and sucking my energy. It caused me great stress since I wasn't doing it. This thought pattern also took me out of being present in the moment with my family. Your story may be like mine, or not, but I'm pretty sure you know what I mean.

The days I took ten minutes to tidy my desk and walked out the door with the essentials always felt the best. I knew what I needed to do in the morning, and it would take me no time at all. Relaxing and enjoying my home time was also more easeful.

If you are feeling depleted, take a few minutes to shift your energy. Stretch your body, walk your students out to the bus and get some fresh air, do ten jumping jacks, do a headstand, or take ten deep breaths to refocus your attention on what is a must-do before you leave. This prevents the aimless wander which sometimes happens when you are in decision fatigue at the end of your day. I would suggest getting into the routine of setting a timer at the end of your school day and tidy up for ten minutes. This will focus your energy and effort so you can leave sooner and feel like you had some closure.

And a reminder, this will be a year-long practice.

Where do you start? Choose one night when you do no schoolwork at home. Keep that night sacred and do something else.

What can you take from the suggestions above to shift your energy once your students have left your classroom? Choose one and begin to do it daily. You might even want to practice it with your students before the bell rings, so you all leave a bit more grounded and less rushed.

A Few Things to Remember...

Having daily practices which fuel me has been my ticket to success. So many teachers tell me they do not have time to put themselves first, but you must, or you will end up sick, having chronic inflammation, and feeling unwell. My daily practice boosts my energy and immune system, de-stresses me, and calms my nervous system so I can have fun and find joy in my days on a regular basis.

What activity or action fuels you and gives you energy? Choose one. Pick a time in your day, make an appointment with yourself, and be on time. Even telling others you have an appointment is helpful. Start with a short time frame, such as ten minutes so it doesn't feel overwhelming.

You may also want to come at this from a different angle. What sucks your energy? Stop doing it. For example, if planning and cooking dinner sends you into overwhelm each night or is frustrating, create a meal plan on the weekend with your crew. Then everyone knows the plan, and you can even ask someone else to get it started. If your new routine is to go for a walk for fifteen minutes as soon as you get home from school, ask someone else to take out the ingredients and set the table while you go for your walk.

And know this is also a practice, and the shift in schedule may take some time for those around you to get the hang of it. That's okay; it doesn't need to be perfect. The goal is to give yourself fifteen minutes to decompress and fuel your body and mind and move dinner forward a bit.

Last, remember you are the boss. If your kids give you pushback, put your foot down! Set boundaries; it will be worth it.

Section Two

The Classroom You Lead:
How You Show Up Matters

Section Two: Introduction

When you show up in the day-to-day of your life, you get to decide who you want to be. It is no different when you walk through the door of your classroom. How you manage your classroom gives your students a guide to how they can behave and how they show up each day. The routines you create with your students will be the glue which teaches life skills. Where you place desks and other furniture will communicate your beliefs to those who visit your room. The team you create with the students in your room will make or break how you spend your time.

We have already discussed your personal health to support you in stepping fully into this role. The bottom line is that if you don't treat yourself like your most valuable asset, your ripple effect will not be as impactful. Who do you choose to be? And how do you inspire your students to be their best selves through instruction, daily interactions, conversations, and how you present yourself?

Chapter 5

Classroom Management

Classroom management is the glue that holds the room together and creates space for students to learn physically, mentally, emotionally, and spiritually. If it isn't a safe and brave space where students feel they can take risks in their learning and show up as themselves, some of them will begin to shrink and hide, while others will stand out and thrive, sometimes at the detriment of other students. How you manage your class is also unique to you and what works for you. It isn't a one-size-fits-all approach.

Personal Energy

When you show up in your classroom as the leader, you set the tone for the energy and how the students show up. Feeling strong and confident will radiate out to your students, creating a space for them to show up similarly. You will also give off the energy that you are the boss, and your actions and follow-up will need to align with a boss mentality. This leader energy will let students know they can show up as they are, sometimes a mess because they have nowhere else which offers the care and understanding you do. This is a powerful learning place to create for all your students, and you will need to be on your A-game regularly to create a consistent safe and brave space for them to land. When you are exhausted and carrying too much on your shoulders, you are unable to offer a safe space effectively. It's okay to have days where you are not on your A-game. This models real life and can be great conversations with your students about how you are handling the ups and downs. However, regularly dragging yourself into your classroom is not responsible as it then becomes a choice and a habit.

I spent three years sharing my grade six class with other teachers because I only worked part-time. I loved my students; they were great kids and so much fun. My challenge was they were not always well behaved with the other teachers. I spent a few months feeling frustrated and having chats with them about their choices.

One day I had an aha moment. How they behave with the other teacher is not my responsibility! It is the other teacher's energy which holds the space when they are in the room, not mine. Thank goodness, as it put so much extra strain on my relationship with the students and wasted my time and energy having conversations about respect.

I have a "don't mess with me" energy when it comes to classroom management. I believe students know how to behave in a classroom, and it is something I indirectly teach daily. Holding them accountable for their actions and giving consequences creates an impact you will notice daily, as they know what is expected of them and are more likely to push the boundaries less. Do not be afraid to be tough on them. Kids work best with boundaries they can trust. You are their teacher first, not their friend, because when push comes to shove you are the one responsible for what goes on in your classroom. They need to know how far they can push you. And, as you have probably already experienced, they *will* test you, some of them daily.

When you use your boss energy and mentality to lead your students, you will create an amazing team. Depending on your students and what you have created, they may be able to support you on the days you are feeling a bit off, or they may take advantage of it. There are usually students who push the boundaries because it is who *they* are. And then there are the ones who will give you extra care on those days. You get to teach and model this balance of give and take.

When you have low energy and are not feeling great, it takes more capacity to manage the room; thus it is even more taxing on your nervous system and the students. Would you rather invest a bit of time and energy in yourself or spend that time managing behaviour in the classroom and become even more depleted?

How you present yourself energetically is so important. When you show up depleted, your students know. When you walk into the room with confidence and have a plan, everyone can feel the difference. Think about the students in your classroom and how they show up. Who shows up confident or even cocky? Who shows up timid or reserved? Everyone brings an energy with them when they enter a space.

For most of you, you will know when a student walks through the door if they need a little extra attention for the day by how they present themselves. Are they putting on a good front but feeling awful on the inside? Or are they wearing the terrible on their sleeves? This gives you a good idea of what to expect from them throughout the day. I share this because the opposite is also true. They know when you are struggling too.

How can you set yourself up to have the capacity both mentally and physically to greet your students however they show up and handle your day more easily for everyone to create an optimal learning environment? Take care of yourself first. Give yourself some time with habits which set you up for success and create a team both in and out of the classroom to support you.

Your Turn
Techniques to Shift Your Energy
and the Energy of the Class

✓ Self-Reflection:

- What am I feeling right now: energized, exhausted, annoyed, or excited?
- What is weighing me down right now? Who can I talk to about it?
- What fun and lively activity can I do to the room's energy? Often doing something to shift the room's energy also shifts yours and you don't have to do it alone or be the one who leads.

✓ Movement:

- Ten jumping jacks
- A brisk walk outside
- Ten deep breaths

Ways to Shift Student Energy:

Student self-reflection—Ask purposeful questions so they become aware of the role they are playing in the classroom.

✓ Possible Questions:

- How are you contributing to the classroom in a positive way?
- How do you think your actions affect others?
- Are you part of the problem or part of the solution? How and why?

✓ Winding Down Activities:

- Stretching—ask students what their favourite stretches are
- Two minutes of silence
- Meditation

✓ Adding in Laughter:

- A funny video
- A game like splat
- Having the students lie on the floor with their heads on each other's tummy, then have someone start to laugh

Expectations

I cannot say this enough: If you do not have follow-through with consequences on all fronts, you have lost your students. The ones who are contributing to creating a great space will lose hope as their efforts are not noticed, and the ones who are subtracting from the safe space you are attempting to create will continue to do so if there are minimal or no consequences. You are the boss, the leader, the teacher. You set the boundaries and the tone of everything, from how students treat each other to how papers are handed back. Be consistent and let them know you are in charge.

In the first classroom in which I taught, I had a grade one student say, "Just one more chance, please, Mrs. Murray." This had me realize they knew they could probably get away with it again and I was giving them too many chances. This awareness from a seven-year-old's single question helped me be firmer with the students and let them know I expected them to make good choices and contribute in a positive way to the classroom.

And don't forget to have fun as well. Being strict does not mean you do not have fun. Follow-through can create space for *more* fun. The boundaries are the structure, and the spontaneity and fun can happen because of the container you create.

In setting the tone for your classroom, conversations which share different perspectives of a situation are a powerful tool and help shift behaviours. Yes, I hold my students to a high standard in my classroom around behaviour, who they choose to be, and the assignments they complete. However, I also have grace and understanding they will not get it "right" all the time. Like most things in life, it is a practice. And when you get twenty to thirty-five bodies in a room, there are lots of opportunities for students to be set off by other students. This too is a great life practice. Learning how to deal with other personalities and behaviours in a safe place gives them confidence.

What are your classroom rules? Do they fit with your own beliefs and values? Did you create them with your students or by yourself? This is one of those places where you can have students be a part of the process. When they get to create the guidelines, they understand them and often follow them more.

Your Turn
What Are Your Expectations?

Grab your journal and do a brain dump on your classroom expectations.

✓ How do you expect students to conduct themselves?

✓ How should they speak to other students?

✓ How should they treat other students?

✓ What can they do when they do not agree with another student?

✓ What can they do when they do not agree with you?

✓ What are the consequences for different situations?

✓ When should you involve other adults for extra support?

✓ What do you expect of them when you are away or out of the room?

✓ Now reflect on how you run your classroom. Do your actions align with your beliefs? If not, what needs to be shifted?

A Safe Place

As we have learned over the past several years, mental health is so critical. Creating a classroom that fosters better mental welfare is imperative. Your own mental capacity can reflect what you are teaching your students about it. How you are personally modeling the importance of your own mental health day in and day out for your students is being seen. When you struggle, they know it and feel it.

If you haven't already, find a course in your district or province on mental health for students. It will change how you see your students and may give you more effective ideas on creating a healthy learning space for them. And it also gives you some support for yourself.

Mental health is one of those areas you don't necessarily under-stand until you have experienced a challenge firsthand within yourself and/or a loved one. After I realized I had anxiety, I began to understand and see it in my students. Before that, I failed to know what it was. My anxiety shows up when I pack too many things into one day or over a period of time. It starts out as feeling rushed, then turns into overwhelm and feeling like I don't have time to pause and breathe. I feel my body tense up, and my breath becomes shallow. I also become ungrounded, and my thinking is not as clear. My upper arms sometimes ache. Because I'm now aware of my beginning symptoms of anxiety, I can pause, take a few breaths, ground myself, and make some choices to shift my schedule and my energy. However, there was a time when I just packed more into my schedule instead of slowing down and giving myself the time I needed to reset.

Working with students who have anxiety can be a challenge, as it shows up differently for everyone. How you run your classroom, your seating arrangement (which includes both the placements of the desks or table and the decisions of who sits near whom), along with your response to students, determine the level of safety students may feel. As the teacher and the leader, the energy in the classroom is your duty. Increasing your students' awareness about the energy of the classroom with conversation and examples is a practical way to have them become involved in creating a collaborative and safe place both for those who experience anxiety and other mental health challenges as well as those who don't.

Having discussions about how people feel and the energy of the room is a good place to start. Questions like:

- What is considered good energy?

- How do you create good energy in your classroom?

- What takes away from the good energy?

- What is considered poor energy?

- What does poor energy look like in the classroom?

- How can you, as an individual, begin to shift the energy?

- How can we, as a whole, shift the energy of the room?

Understanding how people see situations differently is powerful. Not all your students will understand someone else's position, and they see it totally differently from the person sitting across the room from them. Aspects such as how they are raised, who they hang out with, their culture, and past experiences will influence how they see and react to a situation. If one person in your room feels safe in a certain circumstance, another person may not. Again, the more conversations you have about perspective will support your students in understanding what it takes to create a safe place, which is another life skill they can acquire in your room.

A Classroom Exercise–Bring in Students' Perspective

Collect several different objects of various shapes and sizes from your classroom which can serve as a still life. Intentionally arrange them so students on different sides of the room will have a different view to draw. Have your students arrange their desks in a circle around the still life. This will provide a variety of views.

Next, stand in the middle of the circle and ask students to describe what they see when they look at you. Purposefully ask pupils who will not see the same features. One student may say, "I see two eyes," while another person may say, "I see one eye," and a third may say, "You don't have any." This can open the discussion for different perspectives based on what they see and how it isn't always the same, even though you do, in fact, have two eyes. However, if you were looking at the back of someone you don't know, you might assume they have two eyes when they may have lost one for some reason. This brings to the conversation the caution of assumptions.

Continue the lesson by putting on some quiet music and allow your students to draw their perspective. I encourage you to join and draw as well.

When you are finished drawing have your students leave their finished pieces on their desks. Invite students to walk around silently and view others' artwork.

When they have returned to their desks ask them what they noticed. Encourage them to not use names of students and to comment on what they saw only.

Chapter 6

Routines and Organization

Using Routines to Drive Structure and Organization and as a Classroom Management Tool

Routines create neural pathways in the brain. When done daily in a safe space, automation can be created. This means your students don't have to pause and think about what they need when they leave their lockers. They know exactly what to grab. This automation comes at different rates for all students.

Taking the time to understand and acknowledge that my son could only do one thing at a time was an adjustment. I can have many things going on at the same time, so I assumed everyone else could do the same. I look back and realize I was giving him grief over something he couldn't do, and I wasn't the only one. So were his dad and his teachers. We all thought he wasn't trying hard enough and just didn't care.

In speaking with our son later, this was a kick in the gut. He was doing the best he could, and he kept getting pushed to do better but didn't have the tools to make it happen. The structure was missing. No matter what he did, it wasn't enough. Now that we know how his brain works, we can speak to what is working for him and team with him for the things he struggles with. He feels so much more confident in what he does, and he doesn't beat himself up as much.

It often fascinates me how we can understand a concept on one level, and then when we experience that concept for ourselves, it takes our understanding to a whole new plane. Organization was never really a focus for me. I could be organized when I wanted to, but I still struggled with the consistency of being organized. It wasn't until we learned that my son could only effectively hold one thought and follow through with it at a time that I began to understand some of the students I taught on a deeper level. This is where routines play a key role. There will be kids in your class who have it all together around organization, and there will be the ones who struggle multiple times throughout their day. Consistent routines are one of the success tickets for all students to build automation.

I sometimes got frustrated with my learners who couldn't "get it." From the experience with my son, I now understand their frustration level of never seeming to get it right, even though they are trying their best. And I also realize the extra pressure didn't help.

When we bring this into the bigger picture of life, it totally makes sense. Does the person who hates cooking and isn't good at it do the cooking in your house? Probably not. The person who has a strength leads it and supports others. Sometimes it shocks me how I can miss the bigger picture because I'm so micro-focused on the smaller stuff. I miss the root of the problem because I'm focusing on the behaviours. This can easily show up in your classroom while teaching because the behaviours are what are disruptive and what we focus on.

Student feedback is a powerful tool. It gives you multiple perspectives about how your class is running. What is working for someone may be the same thing which is not working for others. One of the challenges is to bring it all together so it works for everyone.

This is where you can source information and ideas from your students by asking them questions like, "What is working in our classroom?" "What is not working for you in our classroom?" "What do you find helpful and why?" and "What is not helpful?" Doing this every couple of months keeps you informed of how your students are doing and what they find supportive. It is also a reminder of the uniqueness of all our students. The cookie-cutter method doesn't always work well in the classroom, even though that's how it is intended to run. It can also inspire students to ask for what they need, which is an amazing life skill to teach.

Organization is a time saver. Take the time to teach and practice it over and over and over again. Routines are so key for those who do not have the natural capacity to be organized or avoid organization.

This one hit home for me based on my own astrological chart. Organization and structure are both wants and needs sections under the moon and sun. I didn't fully understand this until I was forty-five. When I think back to the lack of being consistent with my organization and how I could never keep my room neat and clean, I see I needed and wanted to be organized, but something was missing.

This brings me back to my son, who always struggled with organization and needed it. It wasn't until I understood how his brain worked that I realized I had to literally walk him through the process of organizing his binder and give him space where he didn't feel pressured. This needed to happen repeatedly until it was automatic for him. He is the kid who needs the extra time and support to make it happen. Sometimes he still does. And I realized this is something in which he may often need extra support and time without pressure. So, rather than making it wrong that he hasn't figured it out yet, I support him instead.

As a teacher, my colleagues often commented on how organized I was. This surprised me as I didn't *feel* organized. This possibly comes from the ideal I had about what my desk should look like. I even had a student gift me a stackable organizing tray to help me keep my desk tidy. My husband also leaves the top of his desk almost empty every time he walks away from it. Mine doesn't look like that, so I measure myself and say I'm not organized. However, these days, there are fewer layers of paper covering my desk.

This brings me to the skill of organization. I used to think that after five or six years of being taught how to keep a desk clean, kids should be able to do it. This doesn't seem to be true for all students.

We have all had the students who have organization figured out; it comes naturally to them. Their lockers are immaculate; they are often organized in their desk, whether it is something they do automatically or take time to tidy during the week. We are all uniquely different in so many tiny ways when it comes to structure and keeping things organized. Just because it is simple for one student doesn't mean it isn't super stressful for another.

How can we shift our mindset on organization for the kids who need it the most. What can we do to let them know they are not a failure just because they can't keep their things organized? Can we give them the extra time to do it without the added pressure? This has been key for me: not making it wrong with my words or actions because they can't keep their papers and other supplies organized.

Classroom Routines

Basic tools, like a small list of what to bring to class, stuck in their locker at a younger age, can begin to build automation or help them be more organized for learning. Here are some other basics I used in my class to support myself and students.

Beginning of the Year:

- Review how you want their binders to be organized. Some will come to school with them already done, others will not. Show them what you expect so they have an idea and a picture in their head of what to do.

- Make suggestions about how to store pencils and other basics so they are at their fingertips.

- Have a conversation about what goes in their desk, what doesn't go in their desk, and what goes in their locker, if applicable.

- You can even have a bit of fun with it and have some kids show what not to do.

Daily Schedule: On the whiteboard just inside my door, I outlined my day by subject and projects, so the students knew what to expect in their day. This had students checking it to make sure they had what they needed for the day. I often wrote this the night before as it helped me get clarity on my next day in my head. I have also seen teachers have laminated cards with this information on it, so they didn't have to write it out daily.

Entering and Exiting the Building: This is my favourite one! As a middle school teacher, in the winter or when it was wet outside, I had to stand at the bottom of the stairs and tell some kids to take off their outdoor shoes. They were on the cusp of being in high school where this routine was dropped, and they often didn't change their shoes.

What are the expectations of the students when they enter the building? Noise level, behaviours, and self-regulation are a few essentials. And even though they know better, showing up in those sometimes-unsupervised areas is influential as it reminds them of what is expected. Often just an adult's presence and proximity changes behaviour.

Locker: This will depend on the structure of your school and classroom. Do they have a desk in the classroom which is theirs where they can keep their belongings? If not, they will need to bring everything each time they leave their locker, including the correct binder. If they have a desk in the classroom, have them keep the basics in there. Planning monthly locker organization time is helpful for everyone. The students who have a tidy locker can help others, which makes it less of a monster task for those who find organization challenging. And students who feel like they don't have time to keep their locker clean will have the extra help if they choose it and the time to tackle the task. I also recommend doing this in small groups as when everyone is out there at the same time it's louder, more chaotic, and less effective.

Desks: Whether as a group or individual, desk organization can be incredibly helpful. When students can't find their work or basic items like pencils and erasers, it can be stressful and can hold up the whole class. It also puts them in a negative spotlight, showing the rest of the room that they are not on top of their organization. Planning monthly check-ins and desk cleans can support everyone.

Binders: For those who often feel behind, binders can be a nightmare. They just shove their papers in and move on to what is next. Walking through this as a whole class gives everyone time and space to feel like they can start organized and takes away some stress. There will be students who already have this skill. They often follow along anyway, feeling good about themselves because they can support others.

At the beginning of the year, this might need to be a weekly task with a small group of your students who need it. The key is to not make them wrong and to talk about the importance of taking the time and creating automation, so it is less stressful. Inviting them privately to wrap up their task a few minutes early to give them extra time to put their work away correctly can help. Imagine how frustrating it can be to open your binder and be lost before the lesson even starts. This sends them into overwhelm and can cause anxiety, moving them into stress mode and preventing them from accessing their prefrontal cortex or higher thinking skills.

Classroom Jobs: What classroom jobs can your students do? Ask them. Create a list of your own and then have them add to it. Set aside time at the beginning or end of each month to do this with your class. Some of them do not know the process of what it takes to keep a room clean and tidy. Show them. This is one of those essential life skills. When you clean up after yourself and keep your space clean, it shifts the energy of how you feel.

Handing in Assignments: I had one rule for assignment handing in: Never put it on my desk! Use the hand-in bin. As I mentioned earlier, my desk was often a bit of organized chaos. I always told my students that I was never responsible for papers and assignments they put on my desk. It had to go in the hand-in bin. NO exceptions.

How do you want your students to hand in their assignments? On paper? Digitally turned in on the computer? To your email? Be specific and consistent. For digital versions, you can create a two-minute video for them to review, so you are not spending extra time showing them all individually or searching for assignments in different places. One of your tech-savvy students would be happy to do this for you, and it can be used year after year.

Classroom Cleanup: This is a huge one for me, and it is also an essential life skill. I believe the janitors are there to clean the school, not clean up after the students. I also don't believe teachers need to spend their time cleaning up after the students. How do you want your room to look as you walk out for the day? Don't allow your students to leave the room until it is done! Yes, it may mean finishing up five minutes sooner. This takes the pressure off the students to get out the door on time. It teaches them to leave space and time to take care of their possessions and physical space, as well as to respect other adults in the building who do the cleaning.

Chapter 7

Classroom Setup: Physical Space Matters

What are your beliefs about the physical setup of your room? Getting clear on them will help you create a safe and brave landing space that is supportive for both your students and you. Remember, the physical classroom is ever-changing depending on what is going on in your school, current lessons and projects, holidays, and the seasons.

Shifting desks monthly or every couple of months is ideal. Moving desks every week or two is a bit too often as it doesn't give students enough time to settle into the new space and build stronger relationships with those they sit next to. Setting aside some time in your calendar each month to look at your physical space can help you feel less overwhelmed. If you include your students in this conversation, it creates more of a team atmosphere. And you don't have to do it yourself.

Knowing your students benefits this organizational piece because putting the wrong combination close in proximity can create complete chaos. Sometimes it takes a few arrangements to figure this one out, especially if the students are completely new.

How you arrange your desks also creates a different feel to your room. Whether your students are in rows, pairs, or small groups. Moving desks and arranging the room a bit differently every couple of months shakes up the energy, usually in a good way.

Here are a few things to consider as you navigate the physical setup of your room throughout the year. How do your students work best? This may take a bit of exploring. Which students prefer to sit by themselves? Who works well together? Who should sit across the room from one another? Having students in pairs is a great start. This allows you to see the dynamics of your kids. It can also build their capacity to sit in larger groups of four or six. For some students, sitting with people they don't know can cause extra stress. Sometimes this allows them to expand their capacity, and other times it shuts them down. Be aware of these students so you can support them as they build their rapport with others in the room.

As much as friends want to sit together, especially girls, I find that if they are split up, they tend to build other relationships and get to know the rest of their classmates better. It is fascinating for students to be placed beside each other and then learn new qualities and values about other students they think they know. This also seems to eliminate some of the drama which happens between friends. Then when they work together or hang out, they are not exasperated with each other from sitting together all day.

I often include my students in these discussions as it brings ownership of their classroom and the space that is created. It has them exploring their value and generates more buy-in. Being on the planning team gives them valuable organizational skills, and then you don't have to do it all yourself. Managing the physical space in your classroom isn't something to get "right." You can explore, envision, and have fun with it.

Use the five-word exercise as a reference for what you would like to create in the new space as you shift the furniture in your room. If you have already started your school year, also do this with your students and see if you can come up with five words in common that support the energy of the classroom. These five words then become a reference point throughout your year. You can use them as discussion starters as well as reminders when students are struggling to align their behaviours in the classroom. Some students will pick them up right away and keep them in mind as they navigate day-to-day. Others will need to hear and experience them regularly to help them integrate within their environment.

What I love about using the five words is that it gives others permission to ask questions to create more alignment within the room. Be prepared for students to call on you when you are out of alignment with these five words or use them to defend an idea they would like to try.

How Do You Want Your Classroom to Feel?

About two years ago I used Maria Kondo's method to clean up the extra clutter in my house. This was very powerful for me. And what made it even more powerful was to decide ahead of time what I wanted my space to feel like. For example, I want my kitchen to feel clean and organized, so I make sure to put away all the dishes and clean the counters after I cook. I want my bedroom to feel relaxing and cozy, so I make sure to make my bed and put away my laundry. And I want my classroom to feel inspiring and productive, so I make sure to keep it clean and organized.

What do you want your space to feel like? Your home? Your classroom? And how can you teach this to your students? Begin to bring their awareness to what their space feels like.

Your Turn
Get Clear on Your Own Beliefs

Take a moment and write about your beliefs regarding your physical space and how students work best. This is a brain dump, so do not censor it. When you are complete, what jumps out at you from this process?

Here are some other questions for consideration as you plan out the physical space in your classroom:

✓ Where do you want your desk so you can see everyone?

✓ How do you want the other furniture to be arranged?

- Do you want some cozy spaces for the students who feel nurtured and safe in small spaces?
- Do you need your room to be fully open so you can see everyone all the time?
- Do you want your students to have a say in the process?
- Would it be helpful to add furniture?
- Would it be better to get rid of furniture?
- Is there enough space around the high-traffic areas?

✓ What do you want on your walls? What will create the feeling you want in your classroom? Consider color and patterns and the effect they have on students and yourself. Consider the following:

- Reminders of concepts learned
- Teaching tools
- Student work

- A combination of the above

✓ How often do you want to change your decor? Add this to your calendar so you can plan it in. For older grades, students can help by putting stuff up or taking it down. For younger grades, a parent volunteer or older student can help.

Chapter 8

Creating Your Classroom Team and Values

My largest class had thirty-four students, and it was half grade sevens and half grade sixes. The smallest class I taught was thirteen grade seven students. No matter the number of bodies in your room, there is great possibility in creating a dynamic team as you have so many skills in one place. Each student brings unique abilities to every situation which cannot be duplicated by others. Having your students explore their unique gifts through assignments and interaction with others, both in your room and the school, can have them experiencing the value they have at a young age to offer the world. Each experience, good, bad, or neutral, gives them an idea of what they would like to recreate and what they would not like to experience again.

One of the benefits of a small school is knowing your students, especially when you are teaching them for the second year in a row. One year, I had eighteen students whom I taught grade six to, and the next year, they were part of my split class. Within the first two weeks, my new students all had the routines down, as the grade sevens showed up as leaders and let them know how I ran my classroom through actions and words. It was amazing to witness the power of the team within that class. And each of those grade seven students knew they brought value to the team as they shared their experience and wisdom with the other students who didn't know me as a teacher.

It is imperative we directly teach team building to our students as well as model it. Discussions about honesty, trust, kindness, good friendships, work ethic, and doing your best were topics I weaved into discussions on a regular basis. There are so many great examples happening throughout the day in a classroom which model team building. Bringing students' attention to those events helps them be more aware of how collaboration grows.

When I came across Drew Dudley's work on values I really began to understand and intentionally implement them into my life. His work gave me the framework for my own values as well as the language to teach values to others.

Two of the key values which stand out for me are impact and balance. In his book *This Is Day One*, Dudley defines impact as "a commitment to creating moments which cause people to walk away feeling as if they are better off for having interacted with you," and balance as "a commitment to pursuing equilibrium in your own thoughts, actions, and being" (240).

Knowing these are two of my core values has inspired me to live them more intentionally. It has also helped me understand the value I bring to a group. The concept of having a team and understanding the value a student brings is imperative to their self-confidence.

I know that, for myself, there have been days when I question whether I am making a difference in anyone's life, or if what I do even matters. This often includes a hamster wheel of self-doubt in my head, where I feel like I'm not good enough as a teacher, I compare myself to other teachers, and I berate myself for not being up on my marking and planning. These are just a few of the many self-sabotaging thoughts which run through my head. I fall into gap thinking and focus on the negative. Our students do this as well, and it usually goes on in their head, so no one else knows it is happening.

If I went back to the classroom to teach, I would end each day by having the students write down three wins for their day and give them time for celebrating what they have accomplished. I would want them to know and experience that they bring value, and acknowledging wins daily is a great way to build their confidence. This increased courage could invite them to show up when they work in groups as a participant and as a leader.

And once students begin to value themselves, they can show up to be effective friends, classmates, and kids instead of struggling to function each day with the negative weighing them down. All of us want to know we are valued and we matter. In a team, this is crucial as people can step up and bring their value with confidence; they are also more likely to take risks and give their best. This *best* often includes encouraging others to show up and share their gifts in their various groups. As students begin to understand the value they bring, having them involved in decision-making can be very useful. Some classes are good at this, and some need more instruction and practice.

Your Turn
Building Your Team

Here are a few questions to ponder about how you are directly and indirectly teaching team building and the value which each student brings independently as well as collectively:

✓ How do you teach team building in your room?

✓ What resources have you found that work for you?

✓ Where in your day do you have them celebrate their wins, insights, and learnings so they can see where they are being successful?

✓ Do you teach and post values so students may understand which ones they relate to?

✓ Do you weave values into your lessons?

✓ Do your students know what skills and attributes are their assets?

✓ What strengths do you draw on from your students to support the classroom?

✓ Do you acknowledge that distinct strengths are used differently in various situations?

✓ How do you show your students that they are valued?

✓ Are there students you are overvaluing with your praise and behaviour?

✓ Are there students who might feel undervalued?

Leading the Team

Creating a community of belonging takes practice and patience. Letting go of perfectionism is also imperative and an ongoing task. If you happen to have your students for more than one year, they will already understand and appreciate how you create community, so encourage them to be leaders alongside you to support others.

Decisions as a leader, teacher, or parent can be challenging when others are involved. Often there is pressure to get it right. I learned this form of input in making decisions at a conference. It was super helpful for me to categorize what I fully decided, where others had input, and where they could be the decision makers. I use it often.

- You make the decision—you are the leader and decide based on your own authority and knowledge.

- Input is gathered from those involved, and you still make the decision—having conversations with those involved in the situation, and then you as the leader make the decision with consideration of what others said.

- You make the decision together—this is more consensus; discussions are had, then the final decision is made together.

- They get to choose—students choose what works best for them.

Decide what decisions your students get a say in and let them be a part of them. This creates buy-in, more involvement, and better results. It brings it back to the students feeling valued, and it isn't just a make-work project or doing what the teacher wants. Often some of the projects we created in class with my students' input were the best ones. And I didn't have to do all the work in creating them. They also had a good understanding of what to expect, as they had a hand in creating and managing those expectations. This process added excitement and motivation for all of us.

Helping students understand they have an important role to play is key. If they haven't been directly taught how they affect the space and others around them, they may be clueless about it. You are helping them begin to reflect on themselves and bringing awareness around how what they want matters.

Reflection is a powerful tool we sometimes think takes too long and believe there isn't much benefit from. This doesn't have to be the case. Asking the right questions for students to reflect on is essential. It is also an amazing life tool.

Section Three

Your Students

Section Three: Introduction

As you navigate the complexities of having students in your classroom, there are key influences to pay attention to. Sleep directly affects how they show up in the classroom, as does their support system. Get clear on what this looks like for students and how you can learn more about your students to be more effective in your approach. Building awareness around student choices and how they *choose* to behave on a day-to-day basis gives students the practice to see themselves at their best. Lead by example; give students opportunities to be a part of the team and build their collaboration skills. In the realm of relationships, friendships can be challenging to navigate in a room full of students. How do you teach these concepts?

There are high expectations as to what and how you teach your students. Often, it is a struggle to get through your day and get everything done. When I taught, my students were my focus. As a nurturing person who loves to support and guide others, I naturally was in tune with my students and what supported them. This gift allowed me to help my students on the mental-emotional level so they could show up more for their learning.

On the days my students were "off," getting the curriculum done was like slogging through mud. To break up the stuck energy, we would often play a game, head outside for five minutes, or jump up and move our bodies. I always got better results and behaviour challenges were less because of these breaks. And just like us, some of them were off for the full day and didn't get a lot accomplished. Don't make this wrong. Making them feel like they are a failure on these days only drops them down another level. These are the days they need the most support and to know they matter, no matter what.

Chapter 9

Rest and the Nervous System

Just like us, our students need adequate rest. Lack of sleep takes a toll on the nervous system. When your students show up in your classroom tired or exhausted, they usually struggle to function on a basic level. Sometimes, this is a one-off and isn't a big deal, but for some students, this can be their usual state. Where can you begin to weave in the tools to support students on this level because it makes a difference in how your room runs?

My son used to complain about having to go to bed early. He got annoyed when he went to bed at a similar time to his sister, who is six years younger.

"None of my friends have to go to bed this early!" he would say, usually when he was tired.

I would reply, "They do not have me as their mother."

What I noticed about both of my children is that they were much happier and able to handle life when they had adequate sleep. There were also fewer outbursts and less crankiness. They got sick less often, and they could fully step into being their best selves. Since I am the one who supports them through their daily challenges, it is easier to create the habit of winding down and going to bed earlier than to deal with all that comes when they are tired. This is very similar to the adults I know!

If you have children, you are the boss. Have them go to bed so they get enough rest to make your job easier. This also gives you some time and space in the evening for you to unwind from your day.

Several years ago, I traveled to a junior high leadership conference in Alberta. I was a guest speaker, and my topic was sleep. First, I was surprised by how many students attended my session. Second, I was floored they all had similar answers for how and why they thought they were struggling with sleep.

They struggled with:

- Going to sleep.

- Staying asleep.

- Not feeling excited about their day ahead when they woke up.

- Going to bed early.

- Having the time and energy in their day to do what they loved.

- Feeling stressed, daily.

- Feeling overwhelmed by how much they had going on.

Some of the reasons they had for why they thought they were struggling with sleep were:

- Siblings fighting.

- Parents yelling and arguing.

- Too much homework.

- Staying up late on screens.

- Caffeine drinks.

- Daily stress they didn't have control over.

Sadly, most of them did not have many tools in their toolboxes to support them with these challenges, especially accountability. Be that person—add the essential life tools to their toolbox! We know sleep has a significant impact on our ability to thrive. There is lots of research on sleep, and yet we do not prioritize it for ourselves. Based on the information above, it often isn't being provided to children.

How do we support students with their sleep? The health curriculum is a great place to start, and you can do cross-curricular assignments with language arts, which may include research on sleep, rest, meditation, and other habits which support better wellness and the nervous system. Math is also an excellent place to document results of experiments with habits. Graphing sleep, time on screen, and other habit metrics makes it real and gives them tangible results. Using partners or teams for accountability, including rating how they are feeling on a regular basis, can also be included to create more accountability and check-ins for your students.

Self-reflection around cause and effect can be added into journal writing. I feel it is essential to do this regularly, not just have it as a one-off, as it doesn't create awareness of the ripple effect of sleep or accountability. Having different habits as themes each month for a focus is another way to support students in becoming more aware of their habits and how they affect their day-to-day performance. This is often a game-changer for sports kids as they experience and realize the effect it has on their ability to be great athletes.

And because you have them for the bulk of the day in your classroom, you can model the implementation of daily or regular breaks rather than normalizing pushing through.

This is also to nurture you, not just your students. I used to joke with my students that we took an afternoon body break outside daily so we could both stand each other for the rest of the day. It was true; I needed the break as much as they did.

I already mentioned the ripple effect which rest and other habits have on the nervous system and how it can lift us up to have a great day or knock us down. And you already know students can't access their higher thinking skills when they are in stress mode; thus, the extra time you spend building these habits in your students will show up in your classroom in fewer behaviour challenges, more focused on-task time, and happier students. I would say it is definitely worth investing your time in your students' well-being as it gets them adding in self-care at a young age.

Chapter 10

Layers of Support

Communication with parents is powerful, as it creates a stronger team for the student. As the teacher, you set the bar. Your students know what they can get away with and what they need to do. Building a stable team of support for your students gives them a living example of creating healthy relationships.

Building solid relationships with my students allowed me to joke with them about some of the challenges we faced together. As a mom, I always appreciated teachers who really understood my kids and didn't make the curriculum more important. My children knew they could get support with their personal challenges as well as their schoolwork. We didn't always see eye to eye, and I know each struggle they had with their teachers had them building life skills I wasn't meant to teach them. One of the hardest things to do is to step back and let kids learn from experience, whether they are your own children or students in your classroom.

When my son was in grade five, he hit a wall. His teacher didn't let him slide through. This was a tough lesson for us both. I had to step back and let them figure it out. I had several conversations with his teacher to see what I could do as a parent. She was amazing. And I knew this before she became his teacher. This allowed me to lean on him to do his best work and show up. I also had to let him deal with the consequences of his choices. Struggling for two months was the time he needed to get it. If he just did the work which he was very capable of doing, he did well. And it wasn't too hard, nor did he have to sit at our kitchen table for an hour or two each night dragging his feet, hoping he would get out of it.

Being part of a pilot project where we called each child's parent in September to introduce ourselves as their child's teacher opened the door for communication. In this process, the parents were surprised to hear from their child's teacher without them being "in trouble." This neutral connection allowed us to start on a positive note. It also gave us the chance to chat about any questions or specifics they wanted me to know about their child but were not comfortable reaching out to me to ask. This was a bit time-consuming but well worth it. It took me about a week to call five parents each day after school. I didn't actually get to talk to each parent, but I did leave messages for those who didn't answer and invited them to give me a call. Some did, and some didn't. These phone calls were a first step in letting families know I was there for them as well as for their child.

When a student knows there are regular conversations going on between you and their parents, there is less wiggle room for two different stories to be going on at the same time: One between the parent and child and a different one between the teacher and child. It puts everyone on the same page and holds those involved accountable. It also gives the child the opportunity to step up and learn better integrity, instead of playing one side against the other. This relationship can also build a strong team of support fully centered around the student and their learning. Parents also feel more comfortable calling you when they have questions and concerns.

My favourite story of students taking something home and it not being what I said was when I got a call from a parent who said, "My son told me I'm not allowed to pack him pop in his lunch."

I love these! The conversation continued something like this: "Interesting... what I told the whole class is if they bring pop to school, I will not allow them to drink it during class time, which is when we have our snack. They are more than welcome to drink it at lunch, on their own time."

I also mentioned that sugary drinks do not help children focus, sit at their desks when needed, or interact positively with others in the room for the rest of the day.

After chatting with the parent for a few minutes, we had a couple of laughs and agreed that children do not always communicate everything that goes on at school. They have an eleven-year-old perspective, which can have a few key points missing on occasion.

I have had several conversations with parents where I had to share with them the specifics of what I told their child, so they had complete communication and awareness of the situation. And probably most importantly, I did not take it as a personal attack. I showed up at these conversations with curiosity. I then listened and asked questions. Building these prior relationships with parents also makes it easier to have the tougher conversations when they arise, as a partnership with the student's best interest in mind has already been established.

I also find this to be true with my own children. If I already have an established relationship with their teacher, I can reach out at any time to clarify things or just have a casual conversation about how my child is doing. I am not always concerned about their marks as I have access to them. I want to know how they show up in the classroom to contribute to their own learning and the community of the school.

Chapter 11

Intentional Ripple Effect

How can we inspire our students to be the best version of themselves? How can we celebrate their wins and pick them up from their losses, letting them know one is not more important than the other? How can we teach them failure is growth? These are questions I struggle with daily for myself, with my own kids, and the ones I asked myself regularly in my classroom.

Daily teaching of concepts is very effective. And yes, I know there is an assumption that it takes away from curriculum time... and it may. However, I do believe it teaches kids relevant life skills which are essential for success in their lives, now *and* when they are older. Be prepared, I will continue to ask you to question your beliefs and some of the beliefs of the education system.

What impact do you want to have on students' lives? This is so important to look at. Yes, as a teacher, you will have a great impact on your students' lives. Make it intentional.

Life can be a struggle sometimes. So why would we purposefully make it harder? This still troubles me. There are enough challenging times, why do we need to add more just to learn a lesson? How can we light up kids and let them know they are special and that they matter?

For some of you, this comes naturally. Maybe you were one of those kids who someone else lit up, so you get it. Maybe you are someone who felt no one light you up, and you want to be that person for others. Or maybe you just do not get why you would light up kids; they need to work harder and learn their lessons, just like you did. Whatever your beliefs are, pause and take a breath and examine them.

Where do they come from? Who do they come from? More than likely, they will come from more than one person or one experience from your past. How do you want your students to remember you? Know what you are passing along. Be the person who lights them up, as they will encounter lots of others who try to snuff them out. Make your ripple effect matter.

Do a mini experiment with your class. Do something just for fun. Do something just to shift the energy from heavy to light. And it doesn't matter if it is you who is feeling heavy or the students. Notice what the energy in your class is like. Are you pushing through on something, rushing your students to get it done? Notice this effect. What do you want to create in your classroom?

I once had a student tell me after the first week of school that he liked coming to school again. I asked why. He said it no longer felt like there was a noose tied around his neck, dragging him along. I gave him the space to be himself. He no longer had to operate out of fight or flight mode. He began to flourish as a student and as a young man who was able to show up without the constant fear of being made wrong and shamed. These are the kids who we need to celebrate, especially their unique way of doing things, rather than forcing them to fit in with everyone else.

Which teacher do you want to be? The one who adds stress and fear to your students' daily lives? Or will you be the one who sees them for who they are and encourages that person to fully step forward, acknowledging the gifts and abilities they have? How can you light them up each day and bring in joy to stimulate their brains to be excited about life, amid everything else going on?

What are you currently doing that has your students feeling lit up, seen, and heard? Great job! Are there any other activities or ideas you would like to add?

Chapter 12

Choice

Everything is a choice. It is cause and effect. One action creates another, creating a ripple effect. We often teach about consequences through our actions and our words.

The term *consequence* can have a negative connotation to it. It is defined as a result or effect, typically an unwelcome or unpleasant one. Instead, I invite you to teach choice from this cause-and-effect perspective. One action results in another, without focusing on the judgment of good or bad. When you touch something hot, you get burned, which is a super obvious consequence and easy for all ages to understand. As it is if we move our feet and take steps, it moves us forward. If we look at choices from this viewpoint, it can empower our students.

I am responsible for all my choices, good, bad, and ugly. This motivates me, as I get to choose, which means I'm in the driver's seat of my life. I can no longer blame others for what is going on in my life as I decide. I get to oversee my own life. Sometimes I'm not happy with my options, and I still get to choose. I am in control of my choices. Things like choosing to argue with my spouse have an effect. There is also a different effect from hugging him and having compassion using no words. It is often fun to experiment in conversations and just listen. When others expect you to respond in a certain way and you don't, it shifts the energy and the outcome. Begin to consciously show up in conversations knowing you have a choice in how to involve yourself.

I propose we begin to teach students about their own worth with a deeper dive at a young age. Learning about their own value will give them a better understanding of what is important to them and can influence their decision-making. Once young people begin to implement their own values and understand their choices create an effect, they start to see how they fit in the world and where they can add their meaning to situations and opportunities. This has them leaning into more responsibilities and showing up in teams because they know the importance they bring to the table, instead of second-guessing themselves.

What does choice look like in your classroom? Health lessons are always a fun place to practice choice. The scenarios you offer will depend on what age and level of maturity. You can give them something to read or act out where they are given a choice, and there are several outcomes based on what they choose. You might even want your students to come up with the scenarios.

What we want to emphasize here is the consequence or outcome of each choice: positive, negative, or neutral. This gets the brains of your students wiring pathways, so they are more conscious and aware of the ripple effect of their actions. And they can be more aware of the effect based on what they chose. In the heat of the moment, they don't always make the choice that gives them the best outcome, which, in turn, gives them the experience of what that is like. Experiencing the world is what we are here to do. Let them, guide them, and don't make what they do wrong because it wasn't the best choice. They will need practice, over and over and over! The learning they get in a safe place is what will make the difference.

How young people understand their own value will support them in making choices that align with who they would like to become. By guiding them in discovering what they value and by exploring values with them, they then have the vocabulary to speak about what guides them in regular conversation and then consider them in the choices they make. Most people struggle with their own value. Many of them do not see how amazing they are or the impact they have on the people around them. As a teacher, you bring amazing value to the lives of those you teach. Knowing what we value as individuals can support us in making decisions based on our personal values and allow us to see the impact we have. This process begins at a young age. The benefit or downfall of this is that students are very impressionable when they are young. It depends on the people in their lives as to how they discover their own value and values in a positive or negative way.

Chapter 13

Sharing the Responsibility

Sometimes it is easier to just do things ourselves as it gets done "right" and it is often faster in the beginning. It gets done immediately without the extra effort of asking more than once. However, then you have one more to do on your list when it is already full. In your classroom there are often twenty to thirty other bodies who are yearning for experience and an opportunity to help. Invite them to be part of the team, then give them some responsibility. It will be worth the investment to delegate and guide others.

Experience is a dynamic learning tool. I once heard a colleague say that those who do the most work learn the most. A great example of this is having the leadership students whom I worked with do their own shopping for the supplies they needed for their events. I already know how to shop, and I'm sure they do as well. However, having them go through all the steps it takes to organize the event gets them much more experience than watching me do it. When I'm the guide on the side, it leaves space for them to take the lead.

This statement has me thinking about where else teachers could focus their attention and how much students could build skills by taking on some of the behind-the-scenes tasks. As a teacher, I was often looking for more time and space in my schedule. Sharing the responsibilities within the classroom and school with your students would help solve the time challenge while building life skills simultaneously.

For me, grammar was not very interesting to teach. My apologies to all the English teachers out there who love it. To support myself and my students in learning more about grammar and punctuation, I had a morning message on my board each day. Sometimes it gave instructions as to what we were working on, other times it gave them information about what was going on for the day, or it was an uplifting message. I made purposeful errors in it. When the students arrived, they corrected it with a different colored marker, and then we briefly discussed it before we began our day. My students often volunteered to write this message. It was a five-minute job; I could give this task to a student who had fun creating errors throughout it. They were able to deepen their own knowledge of grammar, take ownership of a routine task in the classroom, and feel valued.

So many of you already know the value of creating buy-in and community in your classroom. Over time and in times of higher stress, we sometimes just do it ourselves as we have lost some of our routine and consistency. This is normal. However, it might be less stressful if we were able to let go of our idea of perfection and allow the students to help. When we do this, they can take on responsibilities in the classroom which saves five to ten minutes throughout the day. Students supporting you with five little jobs can save you twenty-five to fifty minutes each day. Your students feel valued and take pride in being a part of a competent team.

Classroom tasks students can help with:

- Morning messages.

- Writing your day's plan on the board.

- Ensuring all chairs are stacked correctly.

- Organizing the books and bookshelf.

- Ensuring the floor is clean; have everyone grab five items off the floor and make it a game.

- Handing back or collecting assignments.

- Erasing the whiteboard.

- Organizing centres.

- Basic end of the day class cleanup. Yes, we have janitors; their job is to clean the school, not clean up after messy students.

I also encourage you to ask your students what job they see around the classroom and school they could help with.

Chapter 14

Collaboration

Some tasks are often done better with someone else, or at least it can be more fun. Therefore, teach students how to be valued team members. How can they support each other? Do they know the value they bring to the room each day? Are they adding to their own toolboxes by encouraging the other members of their team to do their best to grow their abilities?

As someone who loves to learn and values collaboration, I took the opportunity to mentor student teachers. I would not have been as successful with my class of thirty-four if I had not had an amazing second-year student teacher. This is where creating community is so valuable. I never felt alone in the classroom as the students and I were a team. They regularly helped with daily tasks, often without being asked. It was one of those classes where the students meshed well and worked to create a great experience for everyone.

I appreciate it when I'm part of something which gives me words to describe a complex idea. When I was volunteering with leadership students, I was introduced to the term *care factor*. Simply put, if you are passionate about the outcome regarding what you are working on and contributing your ideas to, this means you have a high care factor. It's close to your heart, and you would like your ideas included. And if what you're working on doesn't have a high care factor, you can sit back and be the muscle in the background, which helps move the project forward based on the direction of those who have taken the lead. Communicating this to your team, either way, lets them know what role you might be best suited for.

Give this your attention in group work in the classroom. Students who work in a group argue over ideas as basic as color just to be seen and heard, while others sit back and seem disinterested. Group work is something which happens often in the classroom. Some kids love working together, while others despise it for all different reasons and no amount of forcing and coercing will have them enjoying working in a group unless it is with the right people.

As a middle school teacher, I wish I had modeled using fishbowl more for my students when it came to groups. In the fishbowl structure, a small group of students can sit on the floor and demonstrate a concept while the others sit around in a circle. It allows the students to model something and then you can discuss it as a whole group. Group work was one of the many concepts I just assumed they knew how to do and didn't need as much guidance. Now I see highlighting different situations would have given students the awareness of what might have been going on within the group dynamics. This would have given them better tools to be more effective listeners and advocates for their ideas.

Team projects can be imperative to build students' confidence and performance. The first year I taught grade six, I had four boys who were best friends. They always wanted to work together, but they didn't get much done, nor did they show what they had learned regarding the curricular outcomes, which is what I needed to assess because they often just messed around.

I saw an opportunity in this. In a conversation with them, I told them if they could show me they could be effective in pairs with each other, I would consider having them work in a group of four.

I was real with them and told them they didn't work well together, were not showing me what they knew, and they were not doing their best work. When they argued, I asked them to give me examples. They came up empty-handed.

This turned out to be an amazing incentive for them. They all had good leadership and teamwork skills because of their friendship and involvement in sports. They knew each other's strengths and weaknesses and were not mean about it. It was so amazing to hear the conversation they had while working in pairs.

Sometimes I would hear them say, "We need to get to work if we want to show Mrs. Murray we can work together so we can all work in a group of four."

This often included glancing at me to see if I was paying attention to what they were doing or not doing. I witnessed as they blossomed before my eyes, growing their strengths and encouraging each other. This looked like talking through challenges, using supportive words, delegating tasks, and praising skills. This process took those four boys from being quite disruptive in my class to great team members who often got work done together. They were also able to transfer the skills of self-confidence, leadership, effective communication, and supporting and uplifting others into the other groups they worked in. I am grateful they rose to the challenge of the opportunity we created.

How can you recognize those who collaborate well, directly teach and model the skills to build up your students, and have them see their own value and inspire others to do the same all at the same time?

Listening, responding, supporting, and adding ideas effectively are great group skills to point out using the fishbowl idea for students. Labeling, giving them examples, and encouraging them as they navigate group work will increase their confidence as well as their work quality. Sometimes you purposefully choose who they work with. Other times it is their choice. Allowing those who struggle with group work to sometimes work alone is an effective choice for everyone. As your students build their collaboration skills, they will be able to work effectively with all students. And when challenges do arrive, they will have the tools to work through conflict and competing ideas.

Chapter 15

Navigating Friendships, the Lifelong Journey

Friendships can be complex to navigate in the classroom. At a younger age, we encourage all of them to be kind to each other. Some teachers even tell their students they are all friends. In a conversation with someone, this idea was blown out of the water for me. We know some kids do not mesh, and there is not enough room in the book to write all the reasons.

What do you, as an adult, do with your friends? I often share food. Would you share food with someone who has hurt your feelings or physically hurt you? I know I might not. This is sometimes what we ask kids to do when we have the expectation that we can all be friends. There are people in your life whom you know you will never be friends with. Allow your students to have the same freedom of choice when it comes to their friends. Teach them discernment and to trust their own instincts and build boundaries about how they want to be treated. I do believe we need to teach them to be respectful and kind to each other, knowing there will be times when it doesn't happen. And we can use those as growth moments.

I had a huge aha moment one day when I was dealing with some of the girls in my class who were struggling with their friendship. I realized they were so depleted and had so much going on at home that they didn't have the capacity to respond to their friends who needed some care and attention. And what seemed to happen was they were unkind to their friends because they were struggling so much. This is huge. How many times do those bodies walk into your classroom just needing to be seen and heard by their friends or you, and there isn't the capacity to give it to them? Do they understand the days when they have no available bandwidth and need to be supported? Can they see when others have no capacity and understand when they are exhausted, stressed, and anxious? It can be hard to be a good friend.

I once listened to someone present who mentioned they high fived all their students and said good morning as they entered the room, every morning. This let the student know they were seen. I also witnessed this with the kindergarten teacher across the hall. She would greet her students with a good morning and often an alphabet letter to recognize. Because she was across the hall from me, she also welcomed my students as they came down the stairs to our classroom. Sometimes they would also say the letter or sound she was holding, as she had also been their kindergarten teacher and knew the routine. This is a great pick-me-up, having your first teacher greet you with a smile and so much kindness.

What is your morning ritual to uplift your learners when they walk into your classroom or the building to increase their capacity to function for the day? How do you let them know they matter and you are here for them?

Mindset can also be applied here. This may happen more in small schools, and I haven't worked in a large one, so I don't have that context. Sometimes students will have had a previous negative experience with another child, and this is what they focus on for the rest of their school years. Throughout the year, I often encourage, teach, and model giving others another chance. This invites others to see who they are now based on their actions today. Get to know this person rather than assuming things about them based on what has happened in the past.

As a young person, I struggled with friendships. I was often left wondering what was wrong with me, and why those kids did not want to hang out with me. In a workshop, I came across the definition of perfectionism based on Brené Brown's work. Perfectionism is managing what others think of you. This resonated with me, and it fits with the conversation on friendship as well. I just wanted the cool kids to like me. I spent the better part of my high school years attempting to fit in and managing what others thought of me. And I know I'm not the only one. Hindsight being twenty-twenty, there were kids I wish I had hung out with. Looking back, they were the coolest kids because they were such amazing people, and I did not know how to see it, recognize it, and celebrate who they were. I was distracted by the shiny people who I thought would be better friends. Boy, was I wrong.

How do we teach students about friendships? I'm going to come from a female perspective and experience. And I know from a masculine perspective, it might be different. As a forty-six-year-old woman, I have cultivated some amazing friendships in the past five years. I wish I had the skills and confidence I have now when I was a teenager. I don't really remember being taught about how to be a good friend, and I may have been. Attempting to figure out who I was in middle school and high school was an experience in itself. Mixing it with all the others who were also trying to figure it out makes it a roller coaster ride and intimidating to really show up and be yourself, as you are looking for validation and acceptance.

Just like everything else, there are so many ways to teach about friendship. Pause here and appreciate what you have done so far, even if it was not intentional. Sometimes we have teaching moments when we are talking with smaller groups of students outside our classroom door, which we do not carry over to others. Other times, these lessons are so valuable we speak to the larger group about it, keeping confidentiality. Either way, give yourself a pat on the back as you cannot work with students and not teach them about friendships and relationships.

This brings us to intentionally teaching friendships, whether it is in small groups or with the whole class. In experiencing the friendships I have cultivated in the last five years, I have come to realize there is a process that involves vulnerability, trust, and forgiveness. When we are having moments of vulnerability, we often need someone to share with, and those we share with are usually those we trust, our friends. In sharing our vulnerability and rawness, we trust our friends will hold space for us. They will support us by listening and sometimes giving advice. There is also the assumption they will not share our story with others or make fun of us.

This process begins to build deep trust in friendships/relationships. As we step into sharing a moment of vulnerability, what the people around us do with our vulnerability is the telltale sign of deeper trust. If they go and tell other students about our experience, we lose trust. If they make fun of us, we feel hurt and no longer trust them. When they hold space, make us feel better, and use candour and care in their communication in the appropriate places, we begin to build more trust and know we can count on them. And then there is a repetition of this process.

Each time we are vulnerable with our friends, their reactions let us know if we can trust them. With each experience, our friendship grows, and we show up with more vulnerability, knowing they are truly there for us.

Unfortunately, the opposite can also happen. In those moments of vulnerability, we share with those who we think are our friends. They talk about us to other people or are unkind in the moments when we truly needed kindness. The repetition of this process allows us to navigate quality friendships. The bottom line is those who break our trust in these moments of vulnerability are not necessarily the people we can turn to. They are not the people who are going to pick us up, give us a hug, and make our day better. Depending on the situation and relationship, your friend may be having a bad day themselves but can't communicate it or they don't understand why they are being unkind.

Since friendships and relationships are a place for us to practice being ourselves, forgiveness is a key component. When our friends do break our trust on occasion, can we forgive and then begin to rebuild our relationships? Other times it is a sign that we cannot trust them and choose to deepen other relationships instead. This is not a cut-and-dried lesson to teach. It is something we need to understand and live ourselves as adults and then navigate situation by situation with our students to guide them.

It is a process we as teachers can teach. We know sometimes our friends need practice to build their trust. We can teach and facilitate "do-overs" so kids can grow the friendship muscle and have a safe place to practice this skill as they grow up. We can be their guide, knowing it is a journey and trajectory in their life which is ever-changing. We can have regular conversations and implement this into health and other appropriate curricular areas.

I do not think friendship is directly taught like this. I didn't understand this process until I was over forty. So, it is unlikely a twelve-year-old can understand it, never mind articulate it. We need to begin to intentionally teach it, give them the words to use, and give them the place to practice vulnerability, trust, and forgiveness. These qualities will make them more capable in their other relationships as they get older.

We need to see our students as people who are navigating the ups and downs of life, just like us. My concern is we seem to be pumping out students who are overwhelmed and anxious into a society which is always on the go, with limited space and time for them, creating more overwhelm and anxiety. Our education system is creating this. Seeing students as people and using the curriculum as a vehicle that is *not* more important than the well-being of students is essential to shifting this norm. As I mentioned earlier in the book, including students in conversations regularly will support this shift.

Section Four

You Are a Leader:
Own It and Live It

Section Four: Introduction

Being labeled a leader can be daunting or not, depending on how you view it. Your own assumptions and beliefs about leadership, about yourself as the guide, and about those around you will inform how you provide opportunities for your students and people you meet. By diving into your own ideology as a leader, you can begin to unpack your ripple effect.

Our limiting expectations and mindset often hold us back from really stepping into teaching and owning the leadership role we hold as educators. These skills are something we can also teach our students so they understand their own ripple effect when they are vulnerable and real in this world. It is also a reminder that anyone can build the effective skills of a leader.

Chapter 16

Assumptions and Beliefs About Ourselves

We all have thoughts about ourselves, our colleagues, our administration, and our students. It is how we make decisions and choices throughout our lives. Sometimes these assumptions and beliefs get in the way of how we teach and how we treat the people we interact with daily.

Tony Robbins's definition of limiting beliefs goes something like this: The stories we tell ourselves about who we are which hold us back from reaching our full potential. They are often subconscious—we don't even know we have them until someone points them out to us.

Diving into these beliefs and understanding how they affect you as a teacher and a person shines a light on what is out of alignment. It allows you to become more intentional about your actions, what you teach and model, and how you lead. This is a list of some limiting beliefs I've come up with. And remember, the goal is to increase awareness, not be critical of yourself and others. Which ones catch your attention? Which ones are interrupting your ability to be even more amazing? Which ones do you hear or see from others?

List of potential limiting beliefs:

About yourself:

- I am not a good teacher.

- I am not a leader.

- Teachers are always tired.

- I don't have any time to myself.

- I am always behind.

- They have it easier.

- People don't get what it's like to be a teacher.

- I need to do more to impress others.

About your school, staff, and students:

- My school only focuses on sports.

- My administration doesn't support me.

- There is negative energy in the staff room.

- These kids never try their best.

- This family can't get it together.

- This family always struggles.

- No wonder this kid always struggles.

- They will never get themselves organized.

As a leader, what are you inadvertently teaching your students because of your own limiting beliefs?

We all have expectations and theories we have picked up from our own experiences. We also get them from others closest to us as well as those who have influenced us along the way. Are you passing these biases and beliefs along to your students directly or indirectly? Once you begin to unpack your own expectations and suspicions, you become more aware of how they show up and can shift to being more intentional. That is leadership. It also gives you the tools to help your students look at their own limiting beliefs. By understanding your own assumptions and beliefs, you can create a more intentional ripple effect on those you encounter.

Your Turn
What Are Your Limiting Beliefs?

This is a great exercise to do with someone you can confide in privately or you can journal it for yourself. You might only want to answer a few questions at a time. See how it feels. Once you begin, it might just be a big mind dump, so grab your journal and write about what your beliefs are. Don't censor it.

What are your beliefs about:

- ✓ Yourself as a person?

- ✓ How you spend your time?

- ✓ How much of your "free" time should be spent on school?

- ✓ The time you spend with your family and friends?

- ✓ Being a teacher?

- ✓ Other teachers?

- ✓ Your school?

- ✓ The other adults in the building?

- ✓ Students in general?

- ✓ Specific students?

- ✓ Some of the families of your students?

- ✓ The community where you teach?

- ✓ Your own health and wellness?

Now that you have more awareness about your beliefs, both limiting and expansive, which may be undermining you as the amazing teacher and person you are, what can you do about them? Reframe them into something positive. Once you are aware of your beliefs, both positive and limiting, notice where they consciously show up. Notice if your awareness shifts how you view the people you interact with, how you act around them, or what you say to them. You can also reframe your thoughts to have a positive one to counter your limiting beliefs.

Here are a few examples of getting curious rather than making assumptions:

- ✓ "I am not an organized teacher" to "I'm getting better at organization" or "I use _____ to help me be more organized."

- ✓ "The staff in the building are all negative" to "I will connect with _____ today because they lift me up."

- ✓ "This student is lazy" to "I wonder what would inspire this student? What might be going on for them?"

- ✓ "No wonder this student struggles, look at their parents" to "I wonder how I can support this student with boundaries at school. What does this family need? Who can I connect them with to get the support they need? Is it my role to step into, or is there another professional to help them?"

Is Your Target Achievable?

I mentioned the idea of perfectionism and ideals earlier. Discussing ideals and perfectionism on a regular basis with your students is essential as it is obvious many of them feel they are not reaching standards set by society. This sets them up to feel like failures. Some of them will feel this failure constantly throughout their day. How can we teach students to question the ideals and ideas of perfectionism?

One way is to start with what they believe is the ideal student. What do they feel the ideal student should be doing? Having conversations about what is real and what is an ideal can support students in doing their best, as well as owning their unique gifts and limitations. Celebrating these rather than often having students feel like they are falling short of the ideal and therefore failing or not good enough is important. For some students, this happens daily. I am curious to know if some of your students will step up to the plate and give their best work if they know the ideal is not expected of them. Kids are very smart.

The student who knows they will never have a project as good as so-and-so often doesn't even try because they have failed the ideal even before they begin. Starting and continuing the conversation, as well as modeling it, can instill that it is okay for them to show up as the unique human they are, rather than feeling like they need to fit into the cookie-cutter mold so often expected of them. What would happen if all students were regularly invited and encouraged to show up as the vital and irreplaceable role they are here to play in this world, just as they are?

Lowest hanging fruit, aiming for a B-, and Kaizen are all concepts I have learned to support me with my perfectionist mindset. Most people have too much on their plate and sometimes as teachers, we feel what we are doing in schools is more urgent than some of the other responsibilities of students. They are being asked to give 110 percent in sports, at home, and in their job. How can we begin to shift their mindset to support them in dropping this idea they have to get it *all* right *all* the time? Or that they can't ask for help?

As a younger person, I picked up the message that to be strong, I need to be able to do it by myself. Are we teaching how to have autonomy and work in a team effectively? Another angle to consider is how does all of this look for different situations and the many hats they wear? Assessing the different expectations and parameters of various environments will help them develop the skills to discern how to show up in the many roles they play in their lives.

Limiting belief: It is better to know how to do it myself than rely on others.

Deeper truth: Creating a team who supports me is a powerful life skill.

The lowest hanging fruit is a simple one: What is the easiest action step students can take to move themselves forward? This can sometimes seem like a cop-out. However, on the days they are really struggling, it can be an olive branch which helps them step out of whatever rut or struggle they might be facing. Knowing it doesn't always have to be so hard can make the difference between a student losing control, making it through the day, or even rocking their day and feeling confident. Time and time again, students show us how resilient they are. So often they are struggling with something and as their teacher, we are sometimes unaware of the whole situation.

Yes, I totally understand we want them to grow, learn, and overcome their weaknesses. When we can offer them some simple successes, it boosts their confidence and helps them see how they can value themselves. We all have had students who struggle because they never feel good enough. I invite you to take some more intentional action on how they see themselves at a young age so they can deepen their confidence as they grow and learn. And we are modeling this for other students around us. In speaking to the students I taught who are now adults, they let me know they appreciated what I demonstrated in my daily actions as a person rather than what I taught them from the curriculum.

Aiming for the B-. Most students and parents are wanting the A+. There is pressure from all sides, including post-secondary, to get the A+. How can we inspire kids to shoot for the B- with the idea they do not have to be perfect? And how can we inspire them to be their unique self and create their best work?

The school division I worked for changed how they assessed students about midway through my time with them. Students no longer just received a number or letter grade which they really didn't understand to begin with. They knew the higher the number the better they did. Often, they didn't know what they retained or what they didn't grasp from that unit or where to put their focus for the next lesson. When they recognized what they were able to demonstrate and what they didn't remember or understand fully, it supported them in learning more about themselves, their learning style, and the curriculum.

In discussions grades, students often gave themselves a mark lower because they looked at the elements of assessment they missed, rather than what they did well on. Or they gave themselves a high mark because they were cocky or just wanted an advanced or mastery mark. I was able to use the language in the descriptions for student assessment to get curious about their assignments, which then gave them an understanding of where they fit in the continuum of the new grading system. It also gave them a guideline as to what they could work toward in their next assignments.

In the mastery section, one of the prompts for scoring asks, "Did you work independently?" They had to consider whether they asked me a question, or if they'd looked to others for help. Not only did this have them consider their own style of work, but it also outlined what it would take on the next assignment to truly become proficient. The definition of mastery also included, "Can apply learning to complex tasks." This part of the assessment often led to open-ended questions about what made the assignment complex. These discussions supported the students in picking apart the requirements for the assignments so they could really understand what was being asked of them for the current project and then apply it to future tasks.

As their teacher, it also gave me an idea of their mental state and thoughts about their performance on assignments. This is a crucial piece to know and sometimes it is a challenge to discern as it isn't always something students talk about. It also allowed me to address their concerns about their own learning and how they were doing academically, emotionally, and mentally. As a bonus, sometimes students shared what we had talked about with other students to support their understanding of the assessments and what to strive for.

It is very effective for students to learn something, apply it, and then teach it to others. By staying connected to your students, having conversations about their assessment, and naming ideals and expectations, your students can build on their confidence, strive for attainable targets, and know they matter in a group of their peers. It's important to encourage students to focus on their personal growth and development rather than just striving for a high grade. As a leader, you can help your students develop a growth mindset by emphasizing the importance of effort, perseverance, and learning from mistakes. By doing this, you can create a classroom culture where students feel comfortable taking risks and trying new things, which can lead to deeper learning and greater academic and personal success in the long run.

Additionally, by providing specific feedback and guidance to students, you can help them understand their strengths and weaknesses and set realistic goals for themselves. Ultimately, the goal is to empower students to take ownership of their learning and to develop the skills and habits they need to be successful not just in school, but in life.

A Classroom Exercise–Continued Conversations on Perfection and Ideals

Using the definition of ideals from *The Gap and The Gain*, have an open discussion with students about where they show up in their lives. Have them create a poster to remind themselves of these ideals and encourage them to post them in their lockers, bedrooms, and other places where they will be seen. With the students' permission, copy a few posters and display them in your classroom.

Weekly, have conversations about ideals and perfectionism with questions such as the following:

What ideal or idea of perfection showed up in your life that had you second-guessing yourself?

Individually, have students answer on a piece of paper to hand in to you for review so you have an idea of what they might be struggling with. You can possibly add the common themes which arise into another lesson.

In a large group, crowdsource the answers and write them on the board. Unpack a few of these situations that you feel would be supportive for the whole group. This lets the students know they are not alone. It would also be helpful to share some of your own experiences in this conversation. This will let them see the adults in their lives are still working on this skill and it is a lifelong one.

A combination of individual and large group activities could be done by having students write for a few minutes on their own, then pairing them up with a safe partner to share what they wrote. Next, pair two groups of two to make a group of four. Have the partners share each other's answers. The group of four listens and writes down themes and commonalities. Then, one person shares those with the larger group. Depending on what arises and your time frame, it may create a whole class discussion or something you can take into another lesson in other curricular areas. This is a liberating structure called 1, 2, 4, All.

Negative Mindset

What you think matters—it shows up in your energy, your actions, and your words.

As you may have experienced, a school can sometimes be a place which feeds negative thoughts. The good news is you are in control of your thoughts. There are many things you cannot control, such as the kids, weather, other drivers, and how others react. But your mindset is one you can influence, so own your power. Remove yourself from situations or be the person who shifts the energy.

Staff rooms can sometimes be a breeding ground for negativity, other times they are great places to connect and unwind. Some days I ate my lunch in my room as I needed quiet. Other days I needed adult connection. On occasion, I would invite another teacher to have lunch with me in my room or go to theirs. This kept me out of the staff room when I needed it, and I still had good connections. And other days, I would sit in a conversation in the staff room and ask the question, "What do you have going on in your life which is amazing?" I did occasionally get funny looks, and sometimes it was uncomfortable. But it was better than listening to someone complain about students and talk about others. I believe it is a responsibility to shift the conversations when they fall into the rut of negativity.

I tend to look on the positive side of things, which helps me see the greatness in the kids, and I would rather focus on how amazing they are. I would not want others talking about me, especially on the days I struggle. You are in control of your own negative thoughts and how you handle them. They may seem too much on some days; talk to someone. Have a healthy vent with someone who knows you need to unpack and unload a situation, making sure you are behind a closed door for these conversations. Set a timer for two minutes. Get it out, and then move on. Often those negative conversations we have about others or have in our head are what suck our energy, and we are not even aware of their power. Become aware of them, make a choice. The ones in your head are the most dangerous, as you are the only one hearing them. Take the lead role in beginning to alter your own thought patterns by choosing the be the change you want to see in the world.

Your Turn
Shift your Negativity

Here are a few questions to bring more awareness to those negative thoughts:

✓ When do you feel the worst during your day?

✓ What thoughts are running through your head during those moments?

✓ What else has happened during the day or week which might be contributing to those thoughts?

✓ Are there others who are triggering those negative thoughts? Are you the person triggering them?

✓ What would you rather feel instead of those negative feelings?

✓ How can you shift your mind to think more positively in those moments?

✓ Who can you connect with to support you in shifting your thinking?

✓ How can you contribute to conversations which shift the energy away from negativity?

✓ What small action step can you take now to treat yourself like your own best friend and counter those negative thoughts?

Chapter 17

Living in Growth Mindset

Just like us, students arrive at the door with assumptions and beliefs about themselves, their peers, the school, and pretty much everything in life. As you teach the curriculum, you begin to learn more about these guiding presumptions by how they interact and conduct themselves. As their leader, you have the influence to begin to unpack these suspicions and beliefs, so students become aware of them. This awareness creates great conversations and debates and has students question things rather than just going along with the status quo.

Critical thinking sets them up to look inward at themselves for growth and take responsibility for the role they play in the classroom and in the world. It also has them making choices for the betterment of themselves and society based on their own values and beliefs.

In speaking with my previous students, I have found that lots of their takeaways and life lessons from my classroom came from the little things I did daily, not the curriculum. This feedback is a reminder to lead the way, not just talk about what might be the best choice. And it's okay to model figuring out the messy as we navigate our own life. This allows students to see a different example.

I thrive on learning new things. Personal growth and discovering different ways to show up in this world as unapologetically me keeps me inspired. As I walk this personal journey, I'm always learning about myself, i.e., how I can grow and step into who I'm becoming next. This is challenging and powerful all at the same time.

Often, I'm dissecting my actions and what I believe about myself and others. Anything is possible when you choose to work on yourself and be the best version. The power comes from taking the action of the better version of myself for the long game, rather than the most convenient and easiest route. Surprisingly, the hard stuff is no longer as uncomfortable as it used to be, and I have less resistance around doing it. Taking challenging actions has helped me reach my goals and do things I never thought possible.

This process also has me unpacking my life experiences from the past and the present, noticing where I can facilitate a do-over, and teaching those around me the same skill by leading by example.

Sometimes in the evenings, I'm a cranky bear to my daughter. I can point out what she is doing wrong, and in the same moment, become aware of what I'm doing and still not be able to stop myself. I just need her to get it and stop the behaviour which is driving me crazy. In the moments of reflection, I realize because I'm so tired, I don't have the capacity to have compassion for her and hold space for what she needs. However, the next morning, I'm able to step into a do-over and ask her for help. I can ask her to remind me to put up my globe, which is an energetic practice we use to get grounded and present.

I realize in these moments that I am in reaction mode and lacking heart connection. While there are things she could also have done differently, I am not in control of her actions and choices, only mine.

Being in the space of continuous growth creates vulnerability, which is a double-edged sword. It can allow deep reflection and growth. It also has us in a place of emotional and spiritual exposure, which can be uncomfortable and fearful. I do not like the idea of being in fear or that things are scary since I usually do them anyway. I have shifted my language to replace "scary" with "edgy." This helps me know I'm at my growth edge and can take the next step, usually reaching into my community for support.

I do love playing my growth edge. In the past, some people have commented, "I just need to be in what I have going on." I'm getting better at this. When I'm feeling vulnerable, I let those around me know how I'm feeling. Upping my self-care is imperative for me to allow what needs to be processed to take its course. Giving myself permission to take a down day with extra self-care is critical to this journey. We often do not give ourselves the physical, emotional, or spiritual space we need to mend what has gone on in our day, week, or year. It is a great idea to take a day for yourself. Make it sacred, and don't do as much for others. You can even ask others to do things for you on these days. I like to add in an oil massage, maybe even a healing treatment, journaling, a hot bath, extra time in nature, and warm nourishing food. These nurturing steps aid in healing what is going on in my body, mind, and emotions leaving me feeling less depleted and ready to face another day with confidence.

Going back to modeling what we believe, how can we teach our students to take time to care for themselves rather than pushing through and ignoring the signals their bodies are giving them? We have all had days of vulnerability ourselves, and we know how hard they can be. We have also seen our students in those vulnerable places. How can we lead and give ourselves a break and model for the students they matter too and so do we?

I feel there would be less overwhelm and anxiety in our world if we allowed ourselves to believe and taught the students they are their most important asset. It's okay to put themselves first. What beliefs do we need to look at so we can begin to model and teach our students to take care of themselves first? We must be a living example of growth mindset and inspire those around us in the process.

Your Turn
Creating Space for Growth Mindset

Take time out for fun by planning and scheduling it. Trust yourself when you feel the need for a break. In your classroom, humor and laughter are amazing tools to shift energy. One easy action is to take your students to the playground or play tag with them. It requires no planning, equipment, or organization, and students can lead it.

Other ideas include watching a funny video, having a body break in the middle of class, adding a just-for-fun art activity, or asking the students what they would like to do. Keep it simple and easy.

Chapter 18

Your Intentional Ripple Effect

Your ripple effect is created by everything you do. As the leader in your classroom and with your students, what is your current ripple effect? How do you set yourself up to be a successful leader who has a positive impact on students? What intentional daily actions do you already take to lift students up and give them great experiences? Where do you allow them to make mistakes so they know it is okay to not get it "right" all the time? How do you give them feedback to have them be 1 percent better the next time around?

Be Vulnerable and Real

There is a balance between vulnerability and professionalism. Everyone will have their own way of connecting and building these relationships. However, your students are not your friends. Yes, you can have great relationships with them, and some will even last after they have graduated. However, while they are in your classroom, they are not your buddies.

Being real with students has been one of my strategies to support them. This came naturally to me, and it wasn't until someone pointed it out that I realized it was a tool to share with others. When

I learn something new, I do my best to live it. This allows my students to see the vulnerability of trying something new, failing, adjusting, and then trying again. I often take my own learning and pass it along to my students and clients when appropriate. There are so many lessons we seem to wait to teach young people until they are older, when they already have a good idea of what is going on.

When I was considering retiring from teaching, my husband and I were having a conversation in code while my daughter was sitting on my lap. We were discussing my not returning to work. My daughter was five at the time. She looked up at me while I was in mid-sentence and asked if I was going to retire. This is a great example of how kids know what's really going on, and I find it much easier on them if I can give them the words and the truth rather than them trying to figure it out themselves, being way off base, or it causing them undue worry. I believe it is imperative to teach students what they need to know at a young age so they can begin to practice and build relevant life skills.

And maybe you need to begin with those closest to you. Are you being real and vulnerable in your life so those closest to you know what is going on? Have you communicated your current struggles with them? What accomplishments have you celebrated recently? It is okay to begin small here. Begin to share a bit more at a time. This process may strengthen your relationships and build a stronger team of support.

Are there places in your life where you need to step into being vulnerable with your students? Is this a strategy which fits for you right now? Take some time to contemplate this. Possibly you need to start sharing this with those you love first.

What have you learned about yourself and your own life which you can bring into your classroom? Discuss with your colleagues and decide for yourself. As a leader, I believe in being authentic about life and making classrooms as real as possible so that young people are not just waiting for life to happen outside of the classroom. The most powerful tools we teach students are the background skills and attitudes embedded in the curriculum. These are the real-life tools which students can practice in our classrooms and take out into the world.

If I were to return to the classroom, I would directly teach my students values that would support them in stepping into their own leadership roles. While I taught values when I was in the classroom, I believe I now have better tools. One such tool is Drew Dudley's *This Is Day One* book. It has encouraged me to look at my values and opportunities in a different light. By practicing and teaching values to those I work with, I have found that presenting concepts from a different viewpoint creates less resistance.

For example, instead of saying, "This is self-respect," and providing ways to live it, we can look at self-respect through Drew Dudley's eyes and use his action driving questions as a guide. "Self-respect is a commitment to making decisions that recognize four things: 1) You have as much right to happiness as anyone else does; 2) You cannot add value to someone else's life until you have added enough to your own; 3) Your happiness is your responsibility; and 4) Your happiness is not possible without forgiveness."

Drew Dudley's Action Driving Questions for Self-Respect include:

- "What did I do today to be good to myself?"

- "How was I my own best friend?"

- "What did I do today to prioritize my own needs?" (2018, p. 245)

By looking at the definition and action driving questions, students can find ways to be good to themselves, be their own best friend, and prioritize their own needs in their daily lives. Rather than telling them what they should be doing, this approach allows students to reflect on themselves and make their own decisions.

Of course, there will be times when students prioritize their own needs when it may not have been the best decision, and this creates space for more conversations and deeper learning as they continue to build their own capacity as individuals. This guidance helps students become who they want to be now, rather than waiting until they are older.

I embrace the concept of learning something, applying it, and then teaching it to others. When we transfer this to students, it allows them to look at what they are learning with new eyes. Students often take in more when they know they will be teaching it to others. This approach enables all students to become leaders, make mistakes, and learn from them firsthand. Starting with their classmates, students can begin to change the lives of those around them. It is a powerful opportunity for students to teach each other.

Vulnerability in Your Classroom

Vulnerability can be a tricky topic because we want people to feel safe, and exposing yourself and getting a different reaction than you were expecting can be damaging. Being vulnerable and pro-fessional as a teacher is a fine balance. I like to think that being real is the middle ground. Be real with those you teach. Let them know when times are tough. They do not need to know all the details. Also, let them know when you are doing great and celebrate those moments too.

I have found that talking about my experiences and how I feel with my students lets them know that the highs and lows are part of life. All the emotions show up for all of us. Acknowledging that adults have similar struggles is helpful. As a child, I know I thought adults had it all figured out and things were easy for them. Now I'm an adult, I know this is not true. Teach them what armouring up and numbing out are. We all do it. We all need breaks. We all fail at things. Openly talking about it helps others to reach out and ask for help when they need it. Also, seeing we are not the only ones struggling in it all makes a huge difference.

Ways we armour up and numb out:

- Screen time: watching Netflix or TV, playing games on a device
- Reading novels
- Alcohol
- Drugs
- Self-harming
- Avoidance
- Gossiping

One of my biggest challenges about this list is that there are a few on it which I also do for fun, such as watching movies or reading novels. So there are times when I'm taking some downtime and do these activities, and there are other times I'm hiding out in them. Finding the balance is pivotal for me. And I still fall back into the rut of numbing out with them. And I'm allowing it to be a process where I notice but don't get too critical of myself.

To bring this back to vulnerability, you can do this activity with your students to have them become more aware of how they are numbing out and armouring up so they don't have to deal with some of the tough stuff in their lives. Ignoring the hard conversations and situations which need your attention doesn't make them go away; they tend to get worse. Be the leader who gives your students the tools to deal with those tough real-life situations.

Your Turn
Where Do You Numb Out?

To start the discussion, provide a few appropriate examples of how people numb out. It's important to define what numbing out and armouring up mean. Brené Brown has some great content on this topic in her *Dare to Lead* book which you can reference. Depending on the age group you teach, the depth of these conversations and how you lead them may vary.

One option is to have students share in a large group, but only if you've created a safe container for this type of vulnerability. Another option is to give students the above question and allow them three to five minutes to answer it on their own. Giving them the option to be anonymous might also be helpful. Then, collect the papers, mix them up, and begin voicing some of the ideas. Depending on the container you've created and your students, you may be able to have them raise their hands if they resonate with what you've read. This can give you an idea of where they are, and it also lets the students know they're not the only ones experiencing this.

The next step is to dive into what they're armouring up about. Depending on your time frame, this can be done in one or several lessons. Ask them what those numbing out techniques are helping them avoid. You can present this question at the same time as the previous question or after. The conversation or lesson will then move to critical thinking as they come up with strategies to solve what they're avoiding. And you might also be ripping a Band-Aid off with these conversations so pay attention to how students are responding and give one-on-one support if needed.

Adding in safe accountability buddies would also be helpful. Have students check in with their partner on how they are doing.

I want to caution you that you might be surprised by how some of your students are numbing out, and they might need professional help. This might be a lesson you do in conjunction with your school counselor or a child development adviser, especially if you teach students who are older than ten.

Leadership Is Not One-Size-Fits-All

You may encounter students in your classroom who possess a wide range of leadership abilities. Just because they do not have these skills at present does not mean they cannot learn them. By having students learn and then teach what they have learned, we can provide young people with the opportunity to practice leadership skills in the classroom and enhance their abilities.

It can be quite discouraging for a student to look at others who are exceptional at leadership and think, "I could never be like them," causing them to give up on trying to become a leader or even put forth their best effort. Leadership is not a one-size-fits-all concept, and there are various kinds of leaders in this world who serve in many different positions. It is vital to teach students they, too, can be leaders. This can sometimes mean allowing the students who have natural leadership abilities to sit down, enabling others to lead. Being a good leader also entails allowing others to take the reins.

When I was attending a leadership conference in New Brunswick, we worked with a gentleman on the waterfront who taught us team building using ropes. He specifically sought input from the quiet leaders. He stated that if everyone were silent, we would be able to hear the fantastic ideas which the quiet leaders had. I loved it. It is crucial to make room for the soft-spoken individuals to speak up.

Some people require an invitation to express their thoughts, and he provided it to them.

What are the different types of leaders in your room? What qualities do they exhibit? How can you inspire quiet leaders and give them opportunities to lead? Do you see all students as leaders? Why or why not? What would need to happen to support the non-leaders to be leaders?

Are You Leading or Just Doing It All?

As the leader in your classroom, you may feel like you need to bring 110 percent to your space. Where can you step back and allow the students to lean into their 15 percent, build life skills, and feel valued? Who is bringing 110 percent all the time? Which kids do not feel like there is space for them to step forward and contribute? Which kids need an invitation? Which students feel like they are not good enough to lead because they think someone else is a better leader than they are? Which students do not like to allow others to lead?

Struggling to do it all left me depleted, exhausted, and resentful of my family. I always felt like I had so much to do and not enough time, especially when it came to keeping my house clean, feeding my family, being a mom, being a wife, and running a classroom. It seemed like I was doing it all. My husband and I used to high-five as we passed each other in the hallway, him going one direction and me going the other. We didn't have time to connect and have a conversation, so this was our connection with a bit of humour. It silently acknowledged we understood we were both giving what we could, we supported each other, and we mattered. This happened during busy times which overlapped, like report cards and calving season, as well as school start-up in the fall and harvest.

During a conversation at a retreat, I realized I had the belief that I *needed* to do it all. I had created my own environment and allowed my team to think I was going to do it all. These were my thoughts, not theirs. In a group discussion unpacking the Liberating Structure of 15 Percent Solutions, I realized I was bringing 110 percent of myself to everything. This left no room for others to step in easily and contribute, and it left me exhausted and depleted.

It has taken me a while to step back, and I continue to do so bit by bit. I began to recognize that each family member was willing to take something off my plate if I let them. I began to see us more as a team, each person with great value and something to contribute. And if I stepped back and didn't charge forward and do it, they were happy to help. It also had nothing to do with the fact that I couldn't do it all. I didn't need to prove I could do it all to show my own value. Another outcome was that my children then had the opportunities to learn essential life skills under my roof.

Great leaders also know when and how to follow. Giving all students the opportunity to lead and be supported is imperative. Your classroom is a great space to practice these skills as it may be the only place they are seen and guided to be leaders.

In the elementary grades, there are often official jobs for students which give them a sense of responsibility, value, and community in their classroom. In the older grades, I found it helpful to include the class in creating the job list and then having them switch the names around each month. My swapping them each week felt like too much work.

From here, how can we carry this forward, making it an ongoing conversation? Let them know they are building their leadership skills. It came to my attention that some of the key concepts we teach kids, we don't spell out for them. We assume they know they are learning them.

In teaching my leadership class, which a hodgepodge of students who came to leadership because it was the best of the worst choices, nothing else interested them, or they were just stuck in this class, I was reminded that all people have leadership skills, some just don't know it.

Showing them directly was a crucial step. One day, a student and I passed kindergarteners playing a game in the hallway. She commented about just having fun games to play instead of learning. I laughed and then pointed out all the concepts the kids were learning from the game. She was astounded as she didn't realize how educational the game was.

As we lead leaders, we need to support them in unpacking some of the obvious things we see and know as adults, as they may not see them. Sometimes we don't even realize all the little lessons packed into what we do daily. Give yourself permission to pause and do some reflection. Including students in this unpacking is so powerful; it begins to change how they look at situations.

I find asking good questions so they can figure out and share what they are seeing and learning is a great way to have them dive deeper into the meaning of what they are doing and understand their ripple effect, increasing their confidence and intentionally impacting others.

What opportunities do you provide your students to lead? Do a brain dump on your own, with a colleague or your team. Celebrate these and borrow ideas from each other. Give yourself permission to implement ideas which might even fail, as failing is often the biggest place we learn. Giving second chances and do-overs is also a great follow-up to failure. You don't have to get it right on the first try. Teaching students this is lifechanging as then they don't see failing in such a negative light.

Questions to ask students when unpacking learning:

- Did you notice...?

- What did you notice?

- Why do you think that is?

- Where else do you see that in the classroom/school?

- How can we use this?

Your Turn
Delegate or Delete

Where in your life are you taking on more than necessary? Where can others step up and support you? It's important to acknowledge that they may not do things the same way you would but allowing them to contribute and bring value can be incredibly impactful. Consider what tasks or responsibilities others can take on to give you more time.

And then how can you bring this conversation to your students? Are they doing it all themselves as well? Who can they get support from? Where can they stop doing something?

Section Five

Implementation
with Your Students

Section Five: Introduction

The tools we use ourselves to feel better can be simple and taught in our classrooms to all ages of students. Where can you take a few minutes in your day to expand everyone's capacity?

Chapter 19

Empowering Students to Navigate Life: Tools for Effective Living

The students in our classrooms are more than just bodies occupying seats. They experience highs and lows like we do and are also affected by what's happening in the world around them. But often, they lack the necessary tools to navigate through these challenges. As educators, it's our responsibility to provide them with the life skills they need to succeed.

The realization I mentioned earlier about middle school students and sleep comes up again. I was surprised to learn many of them were struggling with sleep issues like those experienced by adults. It made me realize while we focus on teaching the curriculum, we may not be supporting them in implementing the tools they need to manage their lives effectively.

We need to ask ourselves some tough questions. Are we contributing to students' overwhelm? Is our education system creating anxious and stressed-out members of society before they even hit eighteen? Are we providing opportunities for them to practice life-sustaining skills which will carry them through the tough times?

If we want to shift this culture, we need to start by having better conversations, modeling good practices, and being open to unpacking situations as they arise in the classroom. Many teachers already do this and deserve accolades for being forerunners in the field. Your efforts will pay off in our future generations.

For five years, I incorporated morning movement and brain breaks into my classroom routine. My students and I would start the day with a ten- to twenty-minute outdoor activity based on Sparks for the Brain, which involved running or walking around the school field. This allowed them to release their energy, get their body systems going, and start the day on a positive note. I also included regular brain breaks and stretches throughout the day, which helped them to self-regulate and de-stress.

As educators, we can help our students develop the skills they need to navigate an ever-changing world. Let's make it our mission to prioritize their well-being and provide them with the tools to succeed.

Hindsight is always twenty-twenty. I wish I had taught my students more about how to be at ease in stressful situations and how simple it can be to calm their nervous systems.

Shortly after leaving my classroom, I volunteered with a group of leadership students and had about twenty minutes with them. I started with two minutes of silence. I was sure they would think it was stupid and push back. But reading the room, I realized they needed more silence and space to just be. They were extremely grateful for the time to pause with no expectations. In our conversations, they communicated how much they had on their plates. Most of them had jobs, home responsibilities, schoolwork, and the difficulties of being a teenager to deal with.

One of the girls was in tears because the pause gave her a moment to realize how much she was doing, and it was too much. She allowed herself to feel her emotional response in her current life situation. This was a pivotal moment for her. Because she was stuck in the go-go of it all, she could not see it was too much. She just put her head down and did what needed to be done, to her own detriment.

If we do not give ourselves and our students the opportunity to slow down, we do not even realize how much we are taxing the nervous system. It is no wonder so many of our students and teachers alike struggle with mental health as they just keep pushing through. It saddens me that this is what we are fostering in our school systems for our students and teachers.

This is where we can lean into a two-for-one. We already feel we do not have enough time in our days to get it all done. In your classroom, you can lead your students to calm their nervous systems and quiet their minds to decrease stress, and you benefit too! The benefit will be twofold: With calmer nervous systems and quieter minds, everyone will be able to interact better, creating more responsiveness rather than reactivity. And both parties can carry this over into their lives outside of the building.

Your Turn
Expanding Capacity and Awareness

Ideas for you and your students to expand your capacity and awareness during the day:

✓ Take the first few minutes of the day to gather as a team and take ten deep breaths. At first, some students might find it silly, especially the younger ones or those who really need it. This can also be done when they come back from recess or another class.

✓ Have students sit for one to two minutes and visualize what they would like to create in their day.

✓ Have students sit for the last few minutes of the day and reflect on:

- Their wins, insights, and learning for the day.
- What they are proud of themselves for.
- Something or someone they appreciated from their day.
- What they are grateful for.

✓ Incorporate morning movement exercises to stimulate the brain and get their systems up and running.

✓ Take a mid-afternoon movement break to re-energize.

These simple activities can help students and teachers decrease stress, increase mindfulness, and promote a positive learning environment.

Chapter 20

Mindfulness and Meditation for You and Your Students

Meditation and breath practices are two tools which can help us shift from the sympathetic nervous system to the parasympathetic nervous system supporting us in recovering from stressful times. They can also help build our capacity to stay more grounded and calmer in the classroom. Meditation can be interchanged with sitting in silence, stillness, and mindfulness, or simply shifting from stress to ease. Sitting in silence is amazing because it allows us to just sit and be quiet without having to do anything else. These moments of stillness and peace offer a break from the constant mind chatter and allow us to be fully present in the moment.

My yoga instructor once described the process of quieting the mind as erasing static from a page. Each time we take a moment of silence in our mind, it erases a spot of static. Over time, those clear spots get bigger and bigger, creating more space for silence and less mind chatter. This, in turn, calms our mind and nervous system more easily.

Incorporating meditation and breath practices into your classroom can benefit both you and your students. Remember, if you do it, your students are more likely to engage as well. This concept is often used with silent reading and writing, and I encourage you to use it with different tools for calming the nervous system.

You may be thinking, *I don't have enough teaching time*. But the truth is, you *do* have time. Giving your students a moment to take a breath and relax can help them shift from fight or flight mode in their nervous system to higher thinking in the frontal cortex. The same is true for you.

Our nervous system is a powerful resource which can either be used effectively or take us out. Before I learned about Ayurveda, I never thought of my nervous system. Now, most of my daily practices, both big and small, are about staying in the rest and digest mode of my nervous system, rather than fight or flight (stress). And you can't be in both at the same time.

I once heard the comparison of one hundred years ago to now. One hundred years ago, we went into fight or flight mode because we were being chased by a wild animal. Now, we have this same response because our computer isn't loading fast enough. This is so true. There are many times in our day when we are triggered into stress mode. Sadly, it has become an expected norm for both adults and students. This is what led me away from my classroom and out of teaching in a school. My nervous system was so fried I couldn't handle the day-to-day stressors of teaching, not to mention adding my regular life and family into the mix. It simply was too much, and I wasn't well. I wasn't willing to continue to compromise my health for my job.

Looking back, I can now see when I was in the midst of it all, I couldn't recognize how sick or stressed I was.

The other day, I was reminded that the effects of the fight or flight response don't just disappear magically. They persist in our system, just as if we had been chased by a tiger and scratched or bitten, we would need to attend to the injury. When our body experiences fight or flight mode, there is a physical impact on all our body systems which we need to heal before we can fully recover. However, these effects are not always visible or obvious.

By incorporating meditation and mindfulness practices into your classroom, you are taking preventive measures which support everyone in being more responsive, increasing their ability to use their prefrontal cortex for higher thinking, and facilitating the digestion and repair of old traumas. Practicing meditations with your students saves you time and allows everyone to feel better, effectively creating a two-for-one scenario.

Your Turn
Start with One Minute

Just begin! Increasing the time you sit in silence, bit by bit, like they do in Daily Five, is a great way to increase everyone's capacity.

Start by sitting quietly for one minute each day, ideally right after recess or gym when they come in all charged up or before they go out, so they will have more capacity to conduct themselves during unstructured times. Have them sit at their desks with their head on their hands and take a few deep breaths. If you teach your own gym class, you can have them lie on the gym floor and then quietly dismiss them one by one or collaborate with your gym teacher.

If you want to double it, have them think about what they are grateful for about the recess or gym class they just had or what they would like to do at recess. As you head into the second week, increase the time to two minutes and so on. If you practice this regularly, it becomes automated for them and requires little to no instruction. They will just do it on their own.

Another option is to create a corner of your room with a desk and noise-cancelling headphones which students can use to self-regulate. When they know they need a few minutes of off time, they can spend some time there. Writing step-by-step instructions will help students arrive at the desk and get settled in right away. If they are feeling unfocused already, this will give them some of the guidance they need without disrupting others.

On an individual basis, encourage students to put their heads on their own desks and take ten breaths to self-regulate or just take a break.

"Stop, Drop, and Meditate" is something else you can add to your classroom routine. When your timer goes off, have the students stop whatever they are doing and sit quietly for two minutes. Then, they can continue with what they were working on.

Conclusion

I see you as you continue to show up in your classroom with a brave face, never knowing what the day will bring.

I see you as you navigate your days with large class sizes and many different personalities in one small room.

I see you as you struggle to find the balance between school and life outside of school.

I see you as you put your students and classroom first.

If you are going to continue in this profession, it is essential to make your physical, emotional, mental, and spiritual health more important than anything else. As I have already mentioned, this goes against the social norm. Be the leader who models a different way for others in your building, both young and old. Taking care of yourself for the long game of life will be worth it. YOU ARE WORTH IT!

In writing this book, I have become much more aware of the complexities of the role a teacher plays and the depth of influence we have with those we encounter in our teaching career. And it isn't always those students you have directly taught. How you show up each day matters. Make that ripple effect, and when you mess up, talk about it; create a do-over, and have grace with yourself and those around you.

I'd also like to acknowledge the vast skillset educators bring to the table on their first day of teaching, which grows day after day and year after year.

Now that you have read this book and possibly have a different perspective, what now?

Reflective Questions:

- What is working in your life?

- What is not working in your life?

- What is one way you can celebrate and acknowledge what is working, possibly with others?

- What is one action step you can take to shift what is not working?

- Who can you enlist for support?

You do not have to do this alone. In fact, it is not meant to be done alone. If you are struggling, know that there is support. If you want to have a conversation about this, sign up for a complimentary session with me through my website.

Get cool emails from
Carman

Talk to Carman

Carman Murray

A retired teacher, Carman Murray is known for her ability to lead others along their transformational journey with both candour and care. After teaching in a classroom for fifteen years she has moved to mentoring women to be their best selves and follow their dreams.

She brings her wisdom as a mom, ranch wife, healer, yoga instructor, and teacher to the groups of women she works with. She brings consistency, accountability, and inspiration to those she impacts. Carman loves being outside and working alongside her husband on their ranch as well as hitting the slopes with her kids.

See more at www.sphericalhealing.ca

Acknowledgements

Thank you to my husband, Ian, for being my best friend, my reality checks when I need them, my quiet strength, and for raising our two amazing children with me.

Thank you to my beautiful children, Amber and Ty, for always being my cheering squad and making sure I make time to play.

Thank you to my parents, Pat and Dan, for encouraging me to follow my dreams as they have changed over the years.

Thank you to my soul sisters Saranjeet, Tammy, and Susan.

Thank you to my family and friends who have encouraged me along the way.

Thank you to the teachers I taught with over the years and all students who I had the opportunity to teach and share a building with. Your impact on my life has been amazing, and I'm so grateful for each and every one of you.

Thank you to Ms. Thomas and Mrs. Gray who inspired me to become a teacher.

And finally, thank you to the GracePoint Team who believed in me every step of the way.

References

Dudley, Drew. 2018. This Is Day One. Hachette Books.

Sullivan, Dan. 2021. The Gap and The Gain. S.L.: Hay House Business.

For more great books from Peak Press
Visit Books.GracePointPublishing.com

PEAK PRESS

If you enjoyed reading *Teachers First,* and purchased it through an online retailer,
please return to the site and write a review to help others find the book.

www.ingramcontent.com/pod-product-compliance
Lightning Source LLC
Chambersburg PA
CBHW072038090426
42733CB00032B/1856